THE COUNSELOR AND THE LAW

Third Edition

By

Bruce R. Hopkins
Barbara S. Anderson

Copyright © 1990 by the American Association for Counseling and Development

American Association for Counseling and Development
5999 Stevenson Avenue
Alexandria, Virginia 22304

Cover Design by Sarah Jane Valdez

Library of Congress Cataloging-in-Publication Data

Hopkins, Bruce R.
    The counselor and the law / by Bruce R. Hopkins, Barbara S. Anderson.—3rd ed.
        p.   cm.
    ISBN 1-55620-076-5
    1. Student counselors—Legal status, laws, etc.—United States.
2. Counseling—Law and legislation—United States.   3. Counselors—
Legal status, laws, etc.—United States.   I. Anderson, Barbara S.,
1952–   II. Title.
KF4192.5.G8H67   1990
344.73′0794—dc20
[347.304794]   90-41913
                                                                          CIP

Printed in the United States of America

CONTENTS

ACKNOWLEDGMENTS

We are grateful to the American Association for Counseling and Development, and to many staff members of AACD, for their continued dedication to the counseling profession that demands that books like this one be produced to guide counselors in their daily practice. In particular, we would like to thank Sylvia Neisenoff of AACD for her assistance in the research for this edition, and Dr. Nancy Pinson-Millburn for reviewing the information about the counseling profession. We would also like to thank Becky Gregory and Dr. Charles Marcantonio for providing hypotheticals drawn from practice, and their insight into the daily situations professional counselors face.

AUTHORS

Bruce R. Hopkins's area of specialization is taxation, with special emphasis on the representation of nonprofit organizations. He serves many nonprofit organizations as general counsel; others use his services as special tax or fundraising counsel. Mr. Hopkins is general counsel of the American Association for Counseling and Development.

He is a professional lecturer in law at the George Washington University National Law Center, teaching the course on tax-exempt organizations. Mr. Hopkins served as chairman of the Committee on Exempt Organizations, Section on Taxation, American Bar Association; chairman, Section of Taxation, National Association of College and University Attorneys; and president, Planned Giving Study Group of Greater Washington, DC.

He is author of the annually supplemented book titled *The Law of Tax-Exempt Organizations* (5th ed., 1987), a book titled *The Law of Fund Raising* (1990), a book titled *Starting and Managing a Nonprofit Organization: A Legal Guide* (1989), and a book titled *Charity Under Siege: Government Regulation of Fund-Raising* (1980). He writes a monthly newsletter for nonprofit organizations titled *The Nonprofit Counsel.*

Mr. Hopkins graduated from the University of Michigan in 1964, and received his law degree from the George Washington University National Law Center in 1967 and a master's of law degree in taxation from the Center in 1971. Mr. Hopkins practices law at Steptoe & Johnson in Washington, DC.

Barbara S. Anderson is a lawyer admitted to practice in Virginia and the District of Columbia. She is a graduate of the George Washington University (BA, 1973) and received her law degree in 1982 from the Washington College of Law of the American University. Formerly in practice with Mr. Hopkins, Mrs. Anderson now writes extensively for a variety of publications, including the *Handicapped Requirements Handbook*, and works on disability and education-related issues in addition to her law practice in Alexandria, Virginia. She is also working on a new book on the Americans With Disabilities Act. Mrs. Anderson was formerly assistant director of the National Association of Student Financial Aid Administrators.

INTRODUCTION

Just 5 years have passed since we put the final touches on the second edition of *The Counselor and the Law*. In that book we attempted, as now, to provide a general guide for counselors to conduct their practice in a legal and ethical manner by outlining the broad legal pitfalls that could trap unwary or un-informed counseling professionals. That the authors and the American As-sociation for Counseling and Development determined a third edition is now necessary highlights a critical aspect of our law: It is a dynamic, ever-evolving process that reflects changes in our society at large, not a stagnant, staid structure that remains the same over time. Of course the essential framework remains intact, but as new situations arise, the law rises to meet new demands and new ideas.

For the counselor, as for lawyers, it is impossible to know all there is to know about the law or to predict the outcome of any case brought to court. We must also emphasize that the law as it applies to counselors varies from state to state and from situation to situation. Court decisions also vary widely depending on the particular judges involved in the case, how well the case is presented, and the particular facts of each case. Nonetheless, professional counselors, as other professionals, have an obligation to keep themselves up-to-date on relevant legal issues affecting them.

We have presented in this work general principles of law to provide professional counselors with a framework of the legal structure affecting them. It is intended as a resource, together with the AACD *Ethical Standards*[1] (in-cluded in Appendix A), the *AACD Ethical Standards Casebook, Fourth Edition*,[2] and other publications yet to come from AACD, to guide counselors in making decisions affecting their professional practice. Many of the hypothetical cases presented in the remaining chapters are drawn from case law in analogous settings and from the *Ethical Standards Casebook*. The principles enunciated in these examples apply to all facets of the counseling profession and should be examined carefully to see how they relate to particular specialties or situations. As with previous editions of this book, our purpose is not to tell counselors how to counsel their clients, but to establish, as clearly as possible, the per-missible bounds of conduct within which the counselor can perform his or her job effectively and legally.

Similarly, this book also is not intended as a substitute for the considered opinion and advice of a lawyer or the lawyer of an employer, who may also be available for advice concerning the particular circumstances of a case in the context of local laws and customs. We must emphasize again that each counselor has the obligation to become familiar with local laws and customs of the profession, as well as the AACD *Ethical Standards*, and to give reasoned, informed consideration to the situations that may present themselves in day-to-day practice.

References

1. American Association for Counseling and Development. (1988). *Ethical standards.* Alexandria, VA: Author.
2. Herlihy, B., & Golden, L. (1990). *AACD ethical standards casebook, fourth edition.* Alexandria, VA: American Association for Counseling and Development.

Chapter 1

THE COUNSELING PROFESSION

An estimated 120,000 to 140,000 professional counselors work in America in a variety of educational and social service settings. Although no specific body of law governs the profession exclusively, courts and state legislatures have made inroads in this area in recent years. Fifteen years ago, when the first edition of this book was published by what was then known as the American Personnel and Guidance Association, the focus was primarily on the potential legal concerns of counselors working in schools. There were few court decisions directly involving school counselors, and even fewer state or federal statutes, to provide guidance as to the limits of permissible conduct toward student counselees. Counselors were viewed by the public, and viewed themselves, as an "emerging profession"; therefore, lacking clear legal direction or a code of professional ethics, many well-meaning counselors ventured into counseling situations with serious ramifications.

At that time, for example, limited school budgets did not support the growing demand for professionals such as school psychologists and social workers, and school counselors increasingly were called upon to fulfill these roles. Because school counselors are not usually licensed to provide therapeutic services, as are psychologists and psychiatrists, this demand for increased services from counselors created a number of potential legal pitfalls. Civil rights and confidentiality problems posed further complications. The heavy emphasis on helping counselees from a humanistic viewpoint, which necessitates a very personal relationship, was also examined as a potential basis for legal liability in cases where a student might be harmed. Finally, the first edition recognized the conflicting responsibilities of school counselors to students, their parents, and society as a whole, of which the school is an important part. These issues were addressed in the first edition of *The Counselor and the Law* to provide some direction to guidance and other school counselors.

The counseling profession of the 1990s is significantly different from the "emerging profession" of the 1960s and early 1970s. Perhaps the most striking differences are in the variety of employment settings where counselors practice and in the types of human concerns with which they now deal. A majority of practicing counselors are still employed by educational institutions, both public and private, but growing numbers of counselors are also found in mental health agencies, rehabilitation agencies, correctional facilities, public employment agencies, community agencies, health care facilities, private practice, business, and industry. They help clients with concerns such as personal and social development, career and educational guidance, mental health, hygiene, physical and vocational rehabilitation, unemployment or underemployment, reentry into school or the work force, substance abuse, family planning and marriage problems, parenting, aging, child abuse, and spiritual concerns. In short, virtually all facets of personal, social, career, and educational needs are addressed by the various professionals who practice under the title "counselor." Most professional counselors have master's degrees in counseling and may also be licensed or certified by the state in which they work, or by a national board such as the National Board for Certified Counselors.[1]

Counseling now enjoys other hallmarks of a mature profession as well. In 1983 the American Personnel and Guidance Association responded most visibly to the growth and change in the profession by changing its name to the American Association for Counseling and Development (AACD). AACD now represents more than 55,000 professional counselors, counselor educators, and other human development specialists in 16 national specialty divisions, with 4 regional assemblies and 56 state branches. In addition to its far-reaching efforts to meet the professional needs of counselors, AACD has also involved itself in other areas that demonstrate the maturity of the profession as a whole. The first is the development, refinement, and expansion of professional ethical standards by which to judge the conduct of counselors, and the establishment of a structure for disciplining members who violate those standards (see Appendix A). A formal procedure for receiving complaints of member misconduct, for conducting impartial hearings and appeals, and for imposing appropriate discipline has been developed and implemented through AACD's Ethics Committee. This voluntary self-regulation by members is widely heralded as a hallmark of an active, mature profession.

Another hallmark is the establishment of a legal defense fund that, in appropriate circumstances, provides limited funds or *amicus curiae* ("friends of the court") briefs to support counselors who are defending a lawsuit. This, too, has been refined and expanded and is now known as the AACD Legal Action Program (see Appendix C). AACD has also implemented a legislative grants program to provide funds to states that are considering credentialing statutes for counselors. Finally, AACD committees and related corporate entities have been created to respond to various external and internal changes in the counseling profession in the areas of licensure, credentialing, accreditation of training programs, government relations, and public relations, to name a few.

What all this means to a counselor faced with any of a wide variety of legal entanglements is this: Counseling is largely viewed today as a mature, diversified profession, with established standards governing the professional conduct of its members. As a result, the conduct of counseling professionals will be scrutinized both from within and without the profession in light of these established standards for preparation, competence, conduct, and, most important, for the care provided to clients.

Note

1. Other certification bodies include the National Academy of Certified Clinical Mental Health Counselors, the Commission on Rehabilitation Counselor Certification, and the National Council for Credentialing of Career Counselors.

Chapter 2

OVERVIEW OF THE LAW AND ETHICS

There is no question that the law has become an all-pervasive part of American society in this century, affecting virtually every aspect of our employment, community, leisure, and even family relationships to some degree. By providing a brief outline of the legal system and some common legal terms and concepts, we hope counselors will gain a fuller understanding of the impact of our laws on the counseling profession, and the issues to be considered when potential problems arise in practice.

Legal issues are to be distinguished from ethical considerations developed by the profession that should be applied in professional practice. This chapter is designed to help counselors understand and appreciate the differences and relationships between the two.

AMERICAN LEGAL STRUCTURE

The American legal system as we know it today evolved from the common law system of England. Our ancestors brought with them from England a detailed code of regulations to govern their behavior that formed the basis for law in the New World. Americans also are governed by the U.S. Constitution, which established our tripartite form of government to initiate, administer, and enforce laws passed by the Congress of the United States (federal laws) and the several states.

Within this structure, laws governing our society derive from two sources: laws passed by governmental bodies such as the Congress or state legislatures, and "rules of law" made by the courts in interpreting the Constitution, federal and state law, and the common law. Law made by courts, sometimes called "judge-made law," takes into account the relevant facts of each particular case, the applicable statutes governing the situation, and decisions from other court cases (called "precedents") that might bear on the facts of the case before the court. This all-inclusive approach to interpreting individual cases results in an ever-changing body of law, within the overall framework of the Constitution, that reflects the changing character of our society.

In appropriate cases courts also consider standards of conduct relevant to a particular profession, as we mentioned in chapter 1. Taking the customary conduct of similarly situated professionals into account when interpreting the particular facts of a case has been an important safeguard for both the public and the affected professionals in many cases.

This all boils down to the concept that our body of laws is dynamic and ever-changing. It is not possible to predict accurately the result of any particular case that might be presented in the future, but rules of law guide the analysis of situations that may develop. It is those general rules of law that we attempt to present in the remaining chapters.

CIVIL LAW AND CRIMINAL LAW

Within this structure there are two distinct types of law: criminal law and civil law. Basically, criminal or penal law includes acts that are prosecuted by the government, not private individuals. Crimes are punishable by fine, imprisonment, or death, and include offenses such as murder, rape, theft, robbery, assault with a deadly weapon, and the like. Individuals can also be prosecuted for aiding and abetting someone who has committed such crimes, or for failing to notify proper authorities in some situations when they have knowledge of such crimes.

Civil law generally includes everything that is not criminal in nature concerning the civil rights of individuals or other bodies. Violations of civil laws are enforced by private persons bringing suit against the violators in a court of law. Most of the law involving counselors falls into this category, which is discussed at length in chapters 3 and 4.

THE COURT SYSTEM

Federal Courts

The federal courts were created by Article III of the Constitution and have the power to hear cases "arising under this Constitution" and the laws of the United States.[1] There are two situations where cases may be brought in federal courts. The first is where the case arises under the laws of the United States, or presents a question of federal law (federal question jurisdiction).[2] The second is where the case involves citizens of different states and the amount in controversy exceeds \$50,000 (diversity jurisdiction).[3] These are the only types of cases that may be heard in federal courts, and the limitation is important. Potential litigants have the option to bring their claims in either state or federal court if the jurisdictional requirements of the federal system can be met.

State Courts

Most state courts are patterned after the federal system, with trial courts, a middle-level appellate court, and a supreme court as the final arbiter of decisions involving state and federal laws that affect the residents of the state. The names of these courts may vary from state to state, but their function is essentially the same. They can hear both civil and criminal cases arising under either state or federal laws, and their decisions are binding on the residents of the state unless overturned by a higher court within the state, or by a federal court.

Appellate Process

In both the state and federal court systems, cases originate in the trial court (called the Federal District Court in the federal system). Both parties put on their case at this level, witnesses are heard, evidence is taken, the relevant law is applied to the facts, and a decision is rendered either by a judge or by a jury. Finally, the judge assigns the appropriate remedies to the parties.

Parties may have the right to appeal decisions of the trial or district court to the intermediate-level appeals court. In the federal system, these 13 courts are called the United States Circuit Courts of Appeal. Their function is to review how the law has been applied to the facts of each particular case and to determine whether the trial court made any errors in its decision that should be overturned, reversed, or sent back to the trial court for additional findings of fact. The state appeals courts generally operate in a similar manner.

Finally, losing parties can request that their case be heard at the third and final level: either the highest court in the state system, or in the federal system, the United States Supreme Court. In addition, cases that have been decided by the highest court of a state may move to the United States Supreme Court through the process known as the "petition for certiorari," or asking the Court to hear the case. The nine Justices of the Supreme Court then vote to decide whether to hear the case and, if at least four Justices agree, the Court will issue a "writ of certiorari" asking that the case be forwarded to the Supreme Court. Cases accepted by the Supreme Court generally involve issues of federal law where decisions of circuit courts on similar issues conflict with one another.

ETHICAL STANDARDS

In addition to the legal considerations that govern the conduct of all citizens, counselors also are guided in their professional conduct by the AACD *Ethical Standards* (1988) (Appendix A). These standards illustrate for counselors "...the behaviors to which they should aspire and give general guidelines for addressing difficult issues."[4] Although these standards are general in nature, they provide an additional source of authority to advise counselors in their daily practice. As set out in the preamble to the standards, "[t]he specification of ethical standards enables the Association to clarify to present and future members and to those served by members the nature of ethical responsibilities held in common by its members."[5] Although not generally enforced by courts of law, ethical standards are enforced internally through the Ethics Committee of AACD. A complaint procedure has been established and penalties for violations of the standards have been set.

Ethical decisions complement the legal parameters but also cover issues that tend to fall into the grey areas, not expressly prohibited, yet not specifically allowed. They take into account the subtle variations of facts in each situation and the reasonable approach to addressing it. The concept of what is ethical also changes with the maturity and perspective of the counseling profession and society at large. For example, as information technology plays a larger role in practice, questions concerning its impact on client confidentiality arise as well. There are no clear answers to all the specific issues as yet, but it is likely that in the future the AACD *Ethical Standards* will address a variety of topics we cannot yet even imagine.

As noted previously, AACD has also published the *Ethical Standards Casebook, Fourth Edition* (1990), "to provide specific examples to illustrate and clarify the meaning and intent of each of the standards."[6] The book presents typical situations a counselor may face in practice and anaylzes the ethical considerations involved in each situation. Counselors are well advised to study the implications of these analyses carefully and to apply the results to their personal practices.

ETHICS AND THE LAW

The ethical standards of a profession are generally enforced through the internal procedures of the professional association, not specifically by courts of law. Yet, in the absence of any clear statutory authority or case law precedent to guide a court in a case involving the conduct of a counselor, courts may apply the standard of care given by other similarly situated professionals, in this case other counselors. Courts may also look to the self-imposed standards of the profession to determine liability. Although no appellate court has yet turned to the AACD *Ethical Standards* for guidance in resolving a case involving counselor conduct, it is possible that this will occur in the near future. Thus, counselors should act in accordance with the standards of counselors in their local community, and thoroughly study and follow the AACD *Ethical Standards* where they apply as a means of avoiding potential liability. Just as courts have utilized the ethical guidelines and standards of care developed by the legal, accounting, and medical professions, a court could find that a counselor has breached his or her professional duty to a client on the basis of the counseling profession's own internal ethical standards.

References

1. U.S. CONST. art. III, §2, cl.1.
2. 28 U.S.C. §1331.
3. 28 U.S.C. §1332.
4. Huey, W. C., & Remley, T. P., Jr., Eds. (1988). *Ethical and legal issues in school counseling.* Alexandria, VA: American School Counselor Association, p. 1.
5. American Association for Counseling and Development. (1988). *Ethical standards.* Preamble. Alexandria, VA: Author.
6. Herlihy, B., & Golden, L. (1990). *AACD ethical standards casebook, fourth edition.* Alexandria, VA: American Association for Counseling and Development, p. 1.

Chapter 3

THE COUNSELOR-CLIENT RELATIONSHIP: PROTECTING CLIENT CONFIDENCES

It is widely recognized that the effectiveness of the relationship between counselor and client hinges precipitously on a fulcrum of trust. Unless the client has complete trust in the counselor, it is unlikely that information can be freely exchanged between the two, and the purpose of the relationship will be frustrated. Complete trust can be established only if the client believes that his or her communications with the counselor will remain confidential.

In its common usage, confidentiality is dependent upon the individuals involved. Without some controlling duty toward a person who shares information, the recipient of that information may keep the confidence as requested or divulge it to others at his or her discretion. At one time or another virtually everyone has "promised not to tell" some secret or confidence. As described in this chapter, however, *confidentiality* is a legal term. More appropriately, it is called *privileged communication*, an exchange of information between two people in a professional-client relationship, in which the confidential relationship has been expressly recognized by statute or by common law. It arises in the context of a proceeding in a court of law, where the professional will not be compelled by the court to reveal protected or privileged client communications.

COMMON LAW BEGINNINGS

The concept originated in the early English common law when it became obvious that clients would not talk freely to their lawyers if they feared their secrets might be revealed in a criminal trial if their lawyer were forced to testify. To promote free exchange of information in this situation, an exception to the rule was carved out prohibiting lawyers from revealing their clients' confidences in court testimony. This privilege was later extended to the husband-wife relationship in the interest of preserving family harmony. No privilege was recognized in early common law for communications between

9

physicians and their patients, or between priests and penitents. But, because these relationships were judged to be dependent upon free and complete communications, they are now sanctioned by state law in many American jurisdictions.[1]

PRIVILEGED COMMUNICATION

Although ethical practice dictates that client confidences not be revealed, except in limited cases (described more fully below), professional-client confidentiality is recognized primarily in the context of raising a "privilege" against revealing information that was disclosed by a client in confidence. *This occurs only when the professional is called as a witness in a court of law.* For the privilege to apply, the communication must have been made in confidence, with the indicated desire that it remain so. This desire need not be explicitly stated, however; a simple action such as closing the office door so that a conversation can remain private would indicate a desire for secrecy. The communication generally must not be made in the presence or hearing of third persons if it is to be judged confidential, unless there is some confidential relationship involving the third person as well, for example an interpreter, a spouse, or perhaps another employee or counselor who is involved with the client.

Over the years the rule of privilege has been narrowly extended to cover other relationships, but it will be recognized by the courts only when it is expressly provided by common law or state statute. For example, Rule 501 of the Federal Rules of Evidence provides that in cases in federal courts, the privilege against testifying will follow the federal common law, as it is interpreted "in the light of reason and experience."[2] In all civil actions and proceedings the federal courts will apply, in most cases, the law of the state where the action arose. But some flexibility is given to courts in determining whether a privilege against the disclosure of communications should be recognized in the absence of a statute granting the privilege. Courts look to a balancing of interests test: Is the public policy of requiring every person to testify to all facts inquired into by a court of law outweighed by the competing public interest in the particular relationship sought to be protected? Four criteria are generally recognized in judging whether the privilege should be granted:

1. The communications must originate in *confidence* that they will not be disclosed.
2. This element of *confidentiality must be essential* to the full and satisfactory maintenance of the relation between the parties.
3. The *relation* must be one which in the opinion of the community ought to be sedulously *fostered*.
4. The *injury* that would inure to the relation by the disclosure of the communications must be *greater than the benefit* thereby gained for the correct disposal of litigation [emphasis in original]. (8 Wigmore 2285[3])

Only if all four of these criteria are present should the privilege be granted. Although the courts generally recognize and apply these criteria in cases before them,[4] judges are reluctant to expand the privileges in the absence of state legislation. State legislatures are also reluctant to broaden the scope of the privileges, which has resulted in an interesting mix of relationships that are recognized as being entitled to confidential privilege. For example, in some states the privilege is accorded the accountant-client relationship, yet denied to counseling agencies and rape victims or to juvenile home staff and juvenile offenders. In New York, the privilege was granted in 1985 to social workers, their employees, and to employees of a social work agency.[5] In other states counselors, and even psychotherapists, are not accorded this privilege.[6] Thus, in states where the counselor-client relationship is not expressly recognized by statute as privileged, a counselor could be required to testify concerning information received from a client. (It should be noted that the counselor's own thoughts and impressions may still be protected, however. See "Reports and Records" in this chapter.)

Within the scope of the Federal Rules of Evidence and Criminal Procedure, the federal courts could further expand recognition of privileged communication so that it would apply to the counselor-client relationship. These rules permit some discretion to the courts, in the absence of legislation to the contrary, to apply the privilege "in the light of reason and experience." State courts with similar procedures may also have wider latitude in extending privileges beyond those expressly recognized by statutes.

Thus, there are two schools of thought concerning the extension of the privilege to the counselor-client relationship. On the one hand, the judiciary probably has the discretion to appraise the relationship, to determine that it meets the four criteria set out by Dean Wigmore as the basis for a confidential relationship, and to rule that communications within such a relationship are to remain confidential. Others believe that this expansion can come only through legislative action, and that those who want to ensure the confidentiality of the counseling relationship must look to state legislatures. Some states have taken the initiative and enacted statutes that guarantee confidentiality in several counseling relationships. A number of states also recognize the privilege for clients of psychiatrists, psychologists, social workers, and sexual assault victim counselors. Counselors are urged to determine the scope of the law of privileged communication in the state(s) in which they practice and to advise clients accordingly.

Given this diversity of thought on the question of confidentiality in the counseling relationship, what should a counselor tell a client who says, "I have a problem I'd like to discuss with you; will you keep it strictly confidential?" The answer depends on a number of things. In the great majority of counseling situations, no information will ever be revealed to the counselor that could become important to a court of law. There need be no restriction to a client, for example, in disclosing incidents relating to self-development. Counselors can tell their clients that they are bound by AACD's *Ethical Standards* (see Appendix A, standard B.2), which state that "the counseling relationship and information resulting therefrom must be kept confidential, consistent with the obligations of the member as a professional person." *Counselors have*

11

the obligation to keep all information relating to the counseling relationship confidential exept when required to testify or provide information to a court of law, or in the limited situations described below.

Furthermore, in states that do recognize the counselor-client relationship as privileged, the counselor may not be forced to testify in a court of law under most circumstances. Counselors should stay alert to changes in the statutes of their states that might affect such privileged communications. They should also keep informed about recent court opinions concerning counselor privileges and of the scope of the privileges allowed by the courts.

WHOSE PRIVILEGE IS IT?

Both the legal privilege and confidentiality clearly belong to the client, and the professional counselor has the duty to protect those client rights. On the other hand, the client may choose to waive the privilege and reveal information on his or her own and can authorize the disclosure of any confidential material to anyone. A counselor is obligated to disclose information when requested to do so by the client, but only information that is specifically requested, and only to the individuals or agencies specified by the client. Many counselors request written authorization from clients before they will provide information. Although this is not a legal requirement, it is a good practice to protect the counselor if a question regarding permission arises later. Counselors, like other professionals, may be held liable for money damages for the *unauthorized disclosure* of confidential client information.

WAIVERS OF THE PRIVILEGE

In addition to the voluntary authorization to waive confidentiality, clients may be held to have waived the legal privilege of confidentiality if they have voluntarily communicated the same information to someone else—for example, a roommate, colleague, or friend.[7]

In some situations the privilege does not apply to client communications. These are incidents where the client initiates an action against the counselor before a state agency, such as a licensing body, or in a court of law in a malpractice action. In effect, the client waives the privilege in these situations by putting his or her *own* condition in issue in the case. Along this same line, a defendant who claims insanity as a defense in a criminal case cannot also claim the physician-patient privilege and withhold evidence of his or her condition because it is relevant to the defense of insanity.

REPORTING CRIMINAL ACTIVITY

Generally speaking, there may be situations where the public interest in disclosure of client confidences outweighs the rights of clients to keep communications privileged. Where a counselor determines that a clear and imminent danger exists to a client or some third person, for example, the counselor clearly has an *ethical* obligation to disclose privileged information to proper authorities.[8] Whether there is a corresponding *legal* obligation to report suspected or potential criminal activity learned in the counseling relationship is less obvious. Some states *require* professionals to report cases of suspected child abuse, for example, but these requirements vary widely from state to state. Counseling professionals may also be required to report potential cases of homicide or suicide. More recent attention has focused on reporting drug abuse and on warning partners of AIDS victims.

Reporting criminal activity revealed in a counseling session may not be a violation of confidentiality obligations in certain circumstances. For example the Missouri Court of Appeals held in 1989 that a psychiatrist's anonymous call to a local crime stoppers unit did not violate the statutory physician-patient privilege. In this case the patient revealed during therapy that she had robbed a service station that day. The psychiatrist revealed only the patient's place of former employment when he called crime stoppers, knowing it would precipitate an investigation. The patient was later arrested and convicted. On appeal, the court upheld the conviction, ruling the psychiatrist had not violated the privilege, because the law creating the privilege applies only to in-court testimony.[9] Here again, it is imperative that counselors determine the extent of the law in the state(s) in which they practice and make a good faith effort to comply with reporting requirements.

DUTY TO WARN?

Despite the privilege recognized for psychotherapists and their clients in some states, the California Supreme Court shocked practicing therapists across the country when it ruled in 1976 that a therapist who knows or should have known that a patient poses a "serious danger of violence" and does not exercise reasonable care to protect the intended victim or notify the police can be held liable (*Tarasoff v. Regents of the University of California*).[10]

This case involved a graduate student at the University of California at Berkeley who revealed in counseling that he intended to kill a young woman, Tatiana Tarasoff, because she had refused his advances. The psychologist considered the threats to be serious and called campus police. They detained Poddar, the student, briefly, but released him because he seemed to be rational. They neither notified the police nor warned Tarasoff. The psychologist also reported his concerns to his supervisor, a psychiatrist, who directed that no further action be taken. Shortly thereafter, Poddar murdered Tarasoff, and her parents sued the psychologist, the psychiatrist, the university counseling center, and the campus police.

The court found that certain duties and obligations arise on the part of a counselor from the special relationship with his or her client and that this "relationship may support affirmative duties for the benefit of third persons." According to the court:

> ... once a therapist does in fact determine, or under applicable professional standards reasonably should have determined, that a

13

patient poses a serious danger of violence to others, he bears a duty to exercise reasonable care to protect the foreseeable victim of that danger.[11]

But the court also noted that the confidential nature of the counseling relationship is critical to its success and ought to be preserved.

> We realize that the open and confidential character of psychotherapeutic dialogue encourages patients to express threats of violence, few of which are ever executed. Certainly a therapist should not be encouraged routinely to reveal such threats; such disclosures could seriously disrupt the patient's relationship with his therapist and with the persons threatened. To the contrary, the therapist's obligations to his patient require that he not disclose a confidence *unless such disclosure is necessary to avert danger to others*, and even then that he do so discreetly, and in a fashion that would preserve the privacy of his patient to the fullest extent compatible with the prevention of the threatened danger.[12]

Consequently, the court concluded that the psychotherapist-patient privilege ought to be preserved, but only to the point where the competing public interest, such as preventing imminent danger to a reasonably identifiable person, intervenes. Of course, this poses a difficult call for the counselor who may have honestly misjudged a client's threats or may have made an unwarranted warning to an intended victim. The counselor might be sued for invasion of the client's right to privacy. To circumvent this, some states have enacted statutes limiting the liability of a counselor in this type of situation. To avoid potential liability, it is important to understand the limits of the *Tarasoff* court's opinion, and any subsequent decisions or legislation in your state.

Tarasoff held that liability would attach where the psychotherapist *reasonably believed, or should have believed* that the client posed a serious danger *to an identifiable potential victim*. In the first instance, the counselor must make the judgment that the client poses a serious danger. Second, there must be an identifiable potential victim. This standard was also used in a New Jersey case, *McIntosh v. Milano* (1979),[13] a Michigan case, *Davis v. Lhim* (1983),[14] and an Illinois case, *Eckhardt v. Kirts* (1989).[15] In the subsequent decision in *Davis v. Lhim* (1988), the Michigan Supreme Court enumerated some factors a mental health professional should consider when deciding whether a client might act upon a threat to a third party. These include the clinical diagnosis of the patient, the context and manner in which the threat is made, the patient's opportunity to act on the threat, the patient's history of violence, the factors that provoked the threat and whether threats are likely to continue, the patient's response to treatment, and the patient's relationship with the potential victim.[16]

The courts, in several cases, have declined to impose liability in the absence of a readily identifiable victim.[17] However, the Vermont Supreme Court ruled that a mental health professional who knows that a patient poses a risk

14

to an identifiable person *or group* has a duty to protect that person or group from danger presented by the patient in *Peck v. Counseling Service of Addison County, Inc.* (1985).[18]

Subsequent courts have held that the duty to warn extends to "forseeable" victims of the client who may not be specifically identifiable, but nonetheless would be likely targets if the client were to become violent or carry through on threats.[19] The Arizona Supreme Court recently used this standard as well, finding liability on the part of a psychiatrist for failing to protect a *foreseeable victim* within the "zone of danger," that is, subject to probable risk of the patient's violent conduct.[20]

The Colorado Supreme Court has gone so far as to reject the "foreseeable victim" analysis altogether, holding that a psychiatrist has a duty to exercise due care to determine whether an involuntarily committed psychiatric patient poses an unreasonable risk of serious bodily harm *to others* if released.[21] In this case a police officer was shot and killed by a former hospital patient who was being escorted out of a convenience store where he had created a disturbance. The court concluded that the releasing psychiatrist had not given due consideration to the propensities of the patient, to extending the term of the patient's commitment, or to placing appropriate conditions on his release.

These cases demonstrate that the courts continue to grapple with the issues of confidentiality and the duty to warn potential victims of violent patients and clients. Therefore, it is critical that counselors stay informed about the legislative and judicial changes in the state(s) in which they practice.

AIDS CASES AND CONFIDENTIALITY

Of all the issues involving a duty to warn on the part of a counselor, perhaps the most difficult involves a client who has been diagnosed with a communicable disease, particularly the human immunodeficiency virus (HIV), or AIDS. In light of *Tarasoff* and subsequent court decisions, do counselors have a duty to warn a sexual partner of an HIV-positive client? The balance between individual privacy and public welfare is indeed delicate in this situation. Unfortunately, there is no clear answer that will cover all cases nationwide because of varying state interpretations of *Tarasoff* and state legislation.

Tarasoff established a duty to "protect" an intended victim from "violence," not to "warn" a consenting adult partner of the risk of transmission of a disease from a sexual act. Even if the decision is extended to the risk of HIV infection, it does not necessarily require warning sexual partners. In Florida, for example, vocational rehabilitation counselors are expressly prohibited from disclosing the fact that a client has tested positive, even to other state or local agencies working with the client. Conversely, counselors may be *required* to warn partners in some jurisdictions, with a corresponding release from liability for such breaches of confidentiality.[22]

AIDS research poses an additional problem for counselors. Public health reporting laws conflict with the duty to maintain confidentiality where researchers are required to report all AIDS cases, and in some states seropositivity to HIV antibodies. Researchers should routinely ensure that broad raw data are not disseminated unnecessarily to agencies to help reduce the possibility of public access to identifying information. Application for a certificate of confidentiality from the U.S. Public Health Service is another means of protecting the confidentiality rights of research subjects.[23] As should be obvious, counselors must carefully research state laws and regulations governing this issue before disclosing such information.

COMMUNICATIONS WITH PARENTS

School counselors are generally bound by the provisions of the Family Educational Rights and Privacy Act of 1974 (FERPA),[24] the implementing regulations,[25] and local state and school board policies concerning disclosure of educational records (see discussion concerning records and reports). Within the context of these controlling provisions, counselors must exercise discretion as to the extent of information to be released to parents from their personal records of confidential counseling sessions. In many cases it is educationally appropriate to discuss the substance of such sessions with parents and teachers, but there may be times when counselors would choose not to do so. Unless compelled by school board policy, however, counselors are not required by FERPA to make available their personal records or disclose the substance of confidential student counseling sessions to parents.

Questions have also arisen concerning contact with noncustodial parents of children and revealing information to them from student records or confidential counseling sessions, particularly when this occurs over the objections of the custodial parent(s). It is clear under the policy of FERPA that, in the absence of a court order to the contrary, noncustodial parents have the same rights to access student educational records as do parents who have custody. This is consistent with the social policy considerations that the parent, even though not having custody of the child, still retains the role of parent and would presumably take custody upon the death of the custodial parent.[26]

Furthermore, it may be imperative that a counselor contact the noncustodial parent in some situations where failure to do so could cause harm to the child. Under *Tarasoff*, counselors have a duty to protect others from harm, which is consistent with the school district's duty to act in the best interests of the child and would require contacting the noncustodial parent to protect the welfare of the child.

GROUP COUNSELING AND CONFIDENTIALITY

Group counseling poses additional problems for maintaining confidentiality. Standard B.2 of the AACD *Ethical Standards* advises counselors to "set a norm of confidentiality regarding all group participants' disclosures." This means the counselor has the affirmative ethical responsibility to explain to the entire group at the outset that everything said within the group is to remain confidential.

Generally speaking, however, the legal concept of privileged communication does not apply to group counseling. Despite the clear indications that such therapy is effective in proper situations, the privilege has not been extended to confidences revealed where more than two persons are present, except where there is a statutory exception. Unless specifically granted by statute, all members of a counseling group should assume that they could be called to testify in court concerning any information revealed to the group in counseling sessions.

COUNSELING PUBLIC OFFENDERS

One of the largest problems facing counselors of public offenders (and to some degree, counselors in other institutional settings) is the persistence of role conflicts that "relate to the custodial orientation of most prisons and other settings in which these counselors work" (Page, 1979).[27] Among the many difficulties such counselors face is adhering to an ethical code that stresses confidentiality. A client may wish to discuss particular problems, such as drug use in prison, which could cost the counselor his or her job if the problems are not revealed to prison authorities. Counselors in prisons and prerelease centers may begin to view their primary responsibility as ensuring that the clients obey the rules and regulations of the workplace and of society. They are also required to report to the courts or prison authorities on their clients' progress. These conflicting roles make it difficult to maintain client confidences. As one observer commented,

> When counselors fail to abide by confidentiality requirements, public offenders who seek counseling generally begin to see counseling as a game. These public offenders begin to present themselves in positive ways to their counselors in hopes of receiving positive recommendations that may favorably affect their lives. Often, they also begin to make other members who might be in a group therapy with them look bad in order to impress their counselor. Unless material presented by clients in counseling is confidential, and unless counselors can be trusted to protect their clients' welfares, counseling services offered to public offenders often become a sham. (Page, 1981, p. 59)[28]

Despite these conflicting job requirements, public offender counselors still have an ethical duty to maintain their clients' confidences, a duty that is essential to the effectiveness of the counseling relationship. Counselors should be sure to disclose to clients the information required to be included in periodic court reports and should clearly inform clients that information relating to criminal activities must be reported. Information included in periodic reports should be limited to the minimum that is requested, and client confidences should be protected whenever possible. Standard B.18 of AACD's *Ethical Standards* (see Appendix A) admonishes counselors who are engaged in a work setting that requires a variation from the general ethical standards, including the standard of confidentiality, to consult with other professionals whenever possible to consider justifiable alternatives. This may provide less intrusive means of complying with job reporting demands while preserving the confidentiality of the counseling relationship.

Prison counselors also encounter periodic threats of violence or harm to others by clients in counseling sessions. As is the situation for a counselor outside a prison, the counselor must first determine if the threats of violence are real, involve a plan and weapons, and can be carried out. In such a case, the *Tarasoff* decision would mandate that the counselor take appropriate action to warn the intended victim(s) or take steps to prevent the client from carrying out the plan (Scott, 1985).[29]

REPORTS AND RECORDS

It is important that counselors understand that there are ethical and legal reasons to maintain accurate counseling records and a corresponding duty to keep such records confidential. Counselors are reminded, however, that circumstances may arise when these records may be required to be disclosed to clients or third parties. Consequently it is imperative that all client records be kept accurately and professionally, and it is recommended that required business records be maintained separately from any clinical notes that may be taken. It has been pointed out that clinical records are not legally or ethically required in most cases unless required by the employing agency (Remley, 1990).[30] Once such records are preserved, however, counselors should understand that they may be disclosed at some future time.

The AACD *Ethical Standards* have several provisions dealing with records and reports. These include not releasing identifying information to others when providing general information concerning counselors' practice (standard A.6), requiring that counselors establish a records retention and disposition policy (standard B.2), and the comment that records may have to be disclosed to a third party in emergency situations pursuant to the "duty to warn" cases (standard B.4).

Standard B.5 admonishes:

Records of the counseling relationship, including interview notes, test data, correspondence, tape recordings, electronic data storage, and other documents are to be considered professional information for use in counseling, and they should not be considered a part of the records of the institution or agency in which the counselor is employed unless specified by state statute or regulation. Revelation to others of counseling material must occur only upon the expressed consent of the client.

Standard B.6 also requires that computer records be limited to necesary and appropriate information, destroyed once they are no longer needed, and that only appropriate persons have access to the records.

These standards together set out the confidential nature of the counseling records that counselors have both an ethical and a legal duty to protect.

Counselors should recognize, however, that the records they create might eventually be disclosed to the client or some third party, whether by consent of the client or by court order. For an overview of appropriate record-keeping guidelines, see the article by Remley in the *Ethical Standards Casebook* (1990), pp. 162–169.

There are three particular situations in which counselors are required to disclose their records. The first was discussed previously, when the counselor has a "duty to protect" an intended victim from a client's violent propensities, or where the counselor believes the client is a danger to him- or herself. Records might be provided to another mental health professional or to an attorney representing the client for use in commitment proceedings.

The second is where the client requests that records be disclosed to some third party, or to him- or herself. Although the counselor creates the records, the client has the right to inspect and obtain copies of the records a professional keeps about the client, and to request that copies be sent to other mental health professionals, insurance companies, or others. As discussed earlier, however, counselors must exercise care not to release information to third parties without the consent (preferably in writing) of the client.

Finally, counselors must make their records available when required by court order, even if they believe this will violate their professional ethical responsibility concerning the confidentiality of the counseling relationship. Certainly they may protest such orders, and advise their clients to do so as well, but counselors may not refuse to comply with a court order.

Counselors who work in schools, colleges, or universities that receive federal funding are bound by the record-keeping guidelines of the Family Educational Rights and Privacy Act of 1974 (FERPA), mentioned previously. Sometimes referred to as the "Buckley Amendment," this law was designed to protect the privacy of students by giving students or their parents the "right to review all official records, files and data related to their children." FERPA also provides that such records not be released to third parties without the written permission of the student or parents.

For purposes of FERPA, educational records generally include all records kept by any employee in an educational institution. However, records made by and kept in the sole possession of a "physician, psychiatrist, psychologist or other recognized professional or paraprofessional acting in his professional or paraprofessional capacity . . ." are excluded from the disclosure requirements of FERPA, except that notes may be provided to other treating professionals or reviewed by a physician of the student's choice (34 C.F.R. sec. 99.3). Maintaining counseling records in a locked cabinet, accessible only to the counselor, should meet this requirement.

COURT APPEARANCES

Counselors may be called to testify in court in a variety of capacities. Whether called as an expert witness, a witness of fact, or a party, the counselor must keep in mind the protection of the client's privacy rights. Although required

19

to answer truthfully the questions posed in court, counselors should not volunteer additional information concerning a client. Furthermore, counselors appearing in court in any of these capacities will be under the direction of an attorney, and should plan to consult in advance with that attorney to discuss planned testimony, as well as any concerns about confidentiality (Blau, 1984).[31]

RECOMMENDATIONS FOR PRACTICE

A counselor's duty to maintain client confidences is clearly central to the development of an effective counseling relationship. Yet counselors may find that duty to be in direct competition with their obligations to report certain criminal activity, to reveal client information in the wake of privacy laws, or to warn potential victims of a client's violent intentions. This chapter has illustrated some of the many situations in which counselors must balance competing duties. It is critical that counsleors make their decisions based on complete, timely information, and on a case-by-case basis. In this rapidly changing area of the law, counselors can protect themselves from potential liability in several ways.

First, counselors should know and follow the AACD *Ethical Standards* to the extent that they apply. Although they do not cover all potential situations, the standards are the best source of information on acceptable conduct for counselors. The advice of other professional counselors may also be instrumental in avoiding possible pitfalls. Many agencies or institutions also have in-house attorneys to advise staff on matters that arise in the course of employment. They should be consulted, where available, for advice concerning specific situations.

Second, counselors should keep records and reports current and accurate and carefully preserve any authorizations from clients for release of information. Clients should be made to understand the concept of confidentiality, its limits under applicable state law, and the counselor's other professional responsibilities as well. It is also important that the staff of the counseling office, including secretaries and student interns, fully understand the concept of confidentiality and abide by its dictates. Clear policies should be developed and followed for the retention and destruction of client records.

Third, counselors should discuss cases only with necessary professionals and other parties in a manner that preserves the confidential nature of the information. Counselors should take care that such conversations are not overheard by other people not directly involved in the care or treatment of the client. If there is doubt as to whether certain information should be disclosed, the matter should be discussed with a supervisor or independent legal counsel before the information is disclosed.

Finally, counselors should consider liability insurance coverage, discussed more fully in chapter 6. Such coverage cannot prevent a lawsuit and possible liability, but it can provide for the payment of legal fees and costs, as well as for damages in the event there is a judgment against the counselor.

References

1. 72 A.L.R.Fed.395 (psychotherapist-patient privilege).
2. Federal Rules of Evidence, Rule 501 (Moore's 1989).
3. 8 Wigmore, *Evidence* §2332 (McNaughton Rev. 1961).
4. For a recent case using this analysis, *see* United States v. Friedman, 636 F. Supp. 462 (S.D.N.Y. 1986).
5. New York CPLR Law §4508 (McKinney 1989).
6. 72 A.L.R.Fed. 395, 401–5.
7. People v. Hawkrigg, N.Y.Law J. 2/17/88, p.28, col 7 (Suffolk Co.Ct. 1988).
8. AACD *Ethical Standards*, standard B.4.
9. Missouri v. Beatty, 770 S.W.2d 387 (Mo.Ct.App. 1989).
10. Tarasoff v. Regents of the University of California, 551 P.2d 334 (Cal. 1976).
11. *Ibid.*
12. *Ibid.*
13. McIntosh v. Milano, 403 A.2d 500 (1979).
14. Davis v. Lhim, 335 N.W.2d 481 (Mich.App. 1983).
15. Eckhardt v. Kirts, 534 N.E.2d 1339 (Ill.App. 1989).
16. Davis v. Lhim, 430 Mich. 326 (1988).
17. Thompson v. County of Alameda, 614 P.2d 728 (Cal. 1980); Leedy v. Hartnett, 510 F. Supp. 1125 (M.D.Pa. 1981); Brady v. Hopper, 570 F. Supp. 1333 (D. Colo. 1983); and Mavroudis v. Superior Court, 102 Cal.App.3d 594, 162 Cal.Rptr. 724 (1980).
18. Peck v. Counseling Service of Addison County, Inc., 499 A.2d 422 (Vt. 1985).
19. Jablonski v. United States, 712 F.2d 391 (9th Cir. 1983); Hedlund v. Superior Court, 34 Cal.3d 695, 669 P.2d 41, (1983).
20. Hamman v. County of Maricopa, No. CV-87-0070-PR (Ariz.Sup.Ct. Jan. 19, 1989).
21. Perreira v. Colorado, 768 P.2d 1198 (Colo.Sup.Ct. 1989).
22. Melton, G. (1988). Ethical and legal issues in AIDS-related practice. *American Psychologist*, *43*, 941–947. [Contains an excellent discussion of the complex considerations of this issue.]
23. Melton, G., & Gray (1988). Ethical dilemmas in AIDS research. *American Psychologist*, 43, 60–64.
24. Family Educational Rights and Privacy Act of 1974, §512, 20 U.S.C. §1232g (1974).
25. Privacy Rights of Parents and Students, 34 C.F.R. §§99.1–99.37.
26. Weiss v. Weiss, 52 N.Y.2d 170, 418 N.E.2d 377 (1981).
27. Page, R. C. (1979). Major ethical issues in public offender counseling. *Counseling and Values*, *24*(1), 33–41.
28. Page, R. C. (1981). Client rights and agency demands: The ethical tightrope of the offender counselor. *Counseling and Values*, *26*(1), 55–61.
29. Scott, N. A. (1985). Counseling prisoners: Ethical issues, dilemmas, and cautions. *Journal of Counseling and Development*, *64*, 272–273.
30. Remley, T. P., Jr. (1990). Counseling records: Legal and ethical issues. In B. Herlihy & L. Golden (Eds.), *Ethical standards casebook* (pp. 162–169). Alexandria VA: American Association for Counseling and Development.
31. Blau, T. H. (1984). *The psychologist as expert witness*. New York: Wiley.

Chapter 4

AVOIDING CIVIL LIABILITY

A successful counseling relationship demands that the client have unquestioned confidence in the counselor. That aspect of this unique relationship spawns a host of duties or responsiblities the counselor must fulfill if he or she is to gain and maintain the client's trust. Hence, these duties and responsibilties are crucial to the counseling relationship itself.

There is also no doubt that, in fulfilling their role, counselors must exercise "due care," or face liability in a civil suit for failing to perform their duties as required by law. Civil liability, stated simply, means that one can be sued for acting wrongly toward another, or for failing to act when there was a recognized duty to do so. Judicial relief is usually in the form of money damages awarded to the injured party.

When one assumes a professional role, one is expected to respect legal standards of professional competence and preparation, and exercise a level of care in dealing with clients, called "due care." For some professional relationships, such as those between lawyers and clients or doctors and patients, a large body of law has produced a fairly accurate delineation of exactly what those standards might include. Although there is not a large collection of pertinent decisions involving counselors, we can draw on existing law as it applies to other professions and relate that law to the counseling situation to establish guidelines for the actions of professional counselors.

For counselors, the primary area within which civil liability is found rests in the law of torts. "Tort" is an interesting word. Few people outside the legal profession ever come in contact with the concept. Brought to England with the Normans, the word "tort" means a wrong that legal action is designed to set right. It is a legal wrong against the person, property, or reputation of another individual, and it can take various forms. It may be the *unintentional* violation of an obligation one person owes to another, such as a counselor's obligation to use all of his or her care and skill in dealing with a client. This violation is called "negligence." Alternatively, it may be a direct, possibly intentional abrogation of some persons' legal rights, such as the invasion of privacy through illegal search. Furthermore, counselors may be held liable for the defamation of a client's character; assault; battery; intentional or unintentional infliction of emotional distress; or other *intentional* torts. A counselor may also face liability for non-torts such as copyright infringement, or breach of contract. These areas also will be explored in greater detail.

23

PROFESSIONAL COMPETENCE

Before discussing the concepts of tort liability further, it is important to understand the concept of professional competence. Just what level of professional preparation and competence is required of a counselor obviously varies depending upon the kind of counseling he or she practices. Four general areas of professional competence were outlined by Robinson and Gross (1986).[1] These include: professional growth through continuing education; maintaining accurate knowledge and expertise in areas of specialization; accurately representing professional qualifications; and providing only those services for which one is qualified. These areas may be investigated by state and professional regulatory boards for varying counseling areas and are supported by the AACD *Ethical Standards.*

For example, the standards specify that "the member neither claims nor implies professional qualifications exceeding those possessed and is responsible for correcting any misrepresentations of these qualifications by others" (standard A.4). Thus if a client calls a counselor "doctor" and the counselor does not possess that degree, the counselor is ethically obliged to bring the error to the attention of the client immediately. The standards go on to state that "Members recognize their boundaries of competence and provide only those services and use only those techniques for which they are qualified by training or experience. Members should only accept those positions for which they are professionally qualified" (standard A.7). As Robinson (1988)[2] explained, ". . . it is not enough to read about or to attend a seminar on new techniques or approaches or special client problems. Only through specific training (advanced educational coursework) and experience (under close supervision) are new skills and areas of expertise developed."

It is crucial that counselors follow these ethical standards and consciously strive to work within the limits of their own professional training. Although this seems to be an ethical position, it is also important from a legal standpoint as part of the analysis of a claim of negligence or malpractice. There is a subtle difference between the terms *negligence* and *malpractice.* In a negligence case it is alleged there was a duty, which was breached, and which proximately resulted in injury to another person. Using a "reasonable man" standard, the courts will look to how a reasonably prudent person would have acted in the same situation to determine if the person who breached the duty should be held liable for the injuries. There is an element of foreseeability implicit in this analysis in that a reasonable person is expected to foresee the probable results of his or her actions, including probable injuries that may result. A similar analysis covers the liability for professional actions.

MALPRACTICE

Malpractice is the term that primarily concerns most professional counselors. "By definition malpractice is *professional* misconduct or any unreasonable lack of skill in the performance of professional duties" (Lovett, 1980).[3] It is im-

24

portant to recognize that professional malpractice is regulated by state law and usually applies only to specified, legally certified, or licensed professionals. Psychiatrists and psychologists are generally specified in state professional malpractice laws, but other counseling professionals may not be included and cannot technically be sued for malpractice. Other counseling professionals, however, can still be held liable for their actions based on a negligence theory, infliction of emotional distress, or other torts. The following analysis of malpractice is therefore applicable to unlicensed counselors as well as recognized licensed or certified professionals.

There are several principal situations in which malpractice has generally been found: (a) the procedure followed was not within the realm of accepted professional practice, (b) the technique used was one the counselor was not trained to use (lack of professional competence), (c) the counselor failed to follow a procedure that would have been more helpful, (d) the counselor failed to warn and protect others from a violent client, (e) informed consent was not obtained, or (f) the counselor failed to explain the possible consequences of the treatment.[4]

In order for a counselor to be held liable in tort for malpractice or negligence, three conditions must exist:

- A duty must be owed the plaintiff by the defendant.
- That duty must be breached.
- There must be a causal link between the breach and the plaintiff's injury.[5]

The "duty" owed by the counselor is premised on the existence of a "fiduciary relationship" between the counselor and client, one that fosters the highest level of trust and confidence. The client has the right to expect the highest level of care from the counselor, and the counselor has the obligation to provide that standard of care.

The primary problem in a malpractice suit is determining which standard of care to apply in order to ascertain whether a counselor has breached his or her duty to a client. Professional malpractice is generally judged by whether a reasonably prudent *counselor* in the same or similar circumstance would have acted in the same manner as the counselor did. If the answer is "yes," liability generally will not be found. However, when the counselor holds him- or herself out as an expert in a particular discipline, that person must then meet the standard of care required of an expert in that area. Psychiatrists will be held to a higher standard of care, for example, than master's level therapists. Unfortunately, as a diverse profession, counseling has little history to apply in judging counselor-client relations and required standard of care. Until such a tradition is defined, the courts will continue to borrow standards from related professions, such as psychology, psychiatry, medicine, or law, to measure counselor performance. Professional codes of ethics and normal practice standards will form the basis of such measurement, but courts will continue to balance the injury to the client against related standards as well.

For example in a 1985 case, *Horak v. Biris*, the Court of Appeals of Illinois held that a licensed social worker engaged in the practice of marriage counseling was required to exercise a degree of skill and knowledge normally possessed by members of the social work profession practicing in the same field. Therefore, he had a duty to both the wife and husband he was counseling to be aware of basic psychological principles such as the "transference phenomenon," the mishandling of which was sufficient to allege a breach of the therapist's duty. The court also held that the husband had standing to bring a *malpractice* action for the social worker's mishandling of the treatment of the wife, resulting in the social worker's becoming romantically and emotionally involved with the wife and having sexual relations with her, because this frustrated the purpose of the treatment, which was to improve the couple's marriage. The husband would also be entitled to recover actual damages for loss of consortium and *emotional distress* if it were proven that there was *intentional* malpractice.[6] It is interesting to note that the court also looked to the state licensing statute and to the code of ethics of the National Association of Social Workers in determining the minimum standards of professional conduct to apply in this case.

In a similar case in Maine (*Rowe v. Bennett*, 1986)[7] the court held that a social worker, employed by a community agency to counsel persons with alcohol-related problems, had a duty to provide care in accordance with the standards of practice applicable to similar professionals engaged in counseling and psychotherapy. In this case the counselor became involved emotionally with her patient's companion, who also came for counseling sessions. Although the social worker referred the patient to group therapy and discontinued individual counseling sessions, the social worker and the companion continued their relationship and began living together a few months later. The "acute reactive depression" the patient suffered was found by the court to have been principally caused by the social worker's breach of duty to her patient.

Generally speaking, counselors can limit their exposure to liability by meticulously following the AACD *Ethical Standards*, keeping informed regarding state and local laws, continuing professional education to keep current on techniques in the field, maintaining appropriate business records, and regularly attending professional meetings. Carrying liability insurance coverage is also recommended for any practicing professional in the event a suit is filed. Even if the counselor is ultimately exonerated, the costs of a trial can be staggering.

Counselors generally deal with clients in individual sessions, group settings, or in crisis intervention. In any of these situations, counselors can be held liable for failing to exercise the requisite skill and care. This is an extremely vague concept, however. What does it mean when a counselor is told that performance will be judged in relation to the degree of skill normally exercised by people with the same professional qualifications? What standards are set for "skill" and "care"? Because the degree of care, the degree of expertise, and the degree of counselor control over the client differ slightly in each of these three major counseling situations, each should be considered separately.

Individual Counseling

No matter what the setting, a one-on-one counseling relationship involves a client who has some problem or difficulty and a counselor who, on the basis of training and experience, works for a solution or a course of action to alleviate the problem. In each case, regardless of the outcome, a professional undertakes to render services to another person, which, under certain circumstances, could form the basis of an action for malpractice. In legal terms, the principle is this:

> One who undertakes, gratuitously or for consideration, to render services to another which he should recognize as necessary for the protection of the other's person or things, is subject to liability to the other for physical harm resulting from his failure to exercise reasonable care to perform his undertaking, if
> a. his failure to exercise such care increases the risk of harm, or
> b. the harm is suffered because of the other's reliance upon the undertaking.[8]

In other words, the counselor is responsible for bringing to the counseling setting the skill and care of a counselor practicing in that area. (See *Horak v. Biris, supra*.) Counselors need not promise specifically that they will conduct themselves in this manner. It is the profession itself that implies that a counselor will do so.

A relatively recent case illustrates this point. In *Bogust v. Iverson* (1960),[9] a Wisconsin counselor was reponsible for "counseling and testing . . . for personal, vocational, educational, scholastic or other problems." His duties also included counseling "those students torn by conflicting feelings, which cause worry and social ineffectiveness" (p.229). Over a 6-month period, the counselor did extensive work with Jeannie, employing aptitude and personality tests. He grew familiar with her personal, social, and educational problems, as well as her conflicting feelings and social ineffectiveness. After extended counseling, he felt Jeannie had made all the progress she could, and he terminated the counseling sessions. Six weeks later Jeannie committed suicide. The counselor was sued by the parents who alleged (a) that the counselor failed to secure emergency psychiatric treatment after he was aware, or should have been aware, of Jeannie's incapacity, (b) that he failed to advise Jeannie's parents of her problem, and (c) that he failed to provide proper student guidance. After considering these allegations, the court ruled the counselor was not liable.

The court did not accept the claim that a duty devolved on the counselor to detect that the student might be contemplating suicide, had become incapacitated, or even that she needed psychiatric treatment. Thus the counselor's failure to advise Jeannie's parents of her problem and his failure to provide corrective guidance were not relevant. Because he owed no duty to perform in any such manner, his failure to do so was not actionable in a court of law, "as a teacher cannot be charged with the same degree of care based on such knowledge as a person trained in medicine or psychiatry could exercise" (p. 230). It is also clear that the court in this case felt that the parents' allegations did not show a breach of duty on the part of the counselor. In other words, the parents would have had to show that a person with the background and training of the average counselor "should have known" that Jeannie was going to commit suicide before he or she could have been held liable.

Another factor in this decision could well be the 6-week lapse of time between the end of treatment and the girl's suicide. A counselor cannot (at least according to this court) be expected to predict that a suicide will take place 6 weeks in the future. So, although a duty existed to use care, the counselor was not held to have breached that duty. Warning signs of impending suicide were held to be beyond his knowledge.

Counselors will not always be excused so easily. Suppose that, in the preceeding case, Jeannie had become extremely agitated when the counselor told her he was terminating the counseling sessions, and had made statements indicating she had suicidal tendencies. In that situation, the failure of the counselor to inform Jeannie's parents or to advise her to seek professional help would likely have been ruled actionable. The counselor's special training probably would be considered to have made him competent to recognize very obvious signs of impending mental or emotional breakdown. A failure then to take action may be held to be a breach of the duty owed to the client. Having thus established a duty, and a breach of that duty, the court could find the counselor liable.

Counselors should consider also the ramifications of the *Tarasoff*[10] decision (discussed in chapter 3) to cases of this nature. In that case, the court ruled that when therapists determine, or should determine, that a patient poses a danger of violence *to another*, they have an *affirmative obligation* to use *reasonable care* to *protect* the intended victim. Presumably this argument could be extended to cover cases where the client poses a clear danger to self as well, giving rise to a duty to take steps to warn those who can effectively protect the client from harming him- or herself. Not all courts would agree to this analysis in cases involving suicide, however, and at least one court (in *Bellah v. Greenson*[11]) specifically refused to extend the *Tarasoff* duty to this situation.

It should also be remembered that the *Tarasoff* decision concerned a psychiatrist with years of extensive training. It could be effectively argued that the case does not apply to other counselors or psychologists, despite the professional training and aspirations of such counselors. On the other hand, the AACD *Ethical Standards* direct all counselors to take action when a "clear and imminent danger" to the client or others is perceived (standard B.4). Notwithstanding the confidentiality obligations, if the counselor perceives such danger, he or she has an ethical obligation to notify authorities, or refer to appropriate specialists. Combined with the *Tarasoff* analysis, such ethical duties could be persuasive to a court in a negligence or malpractice action.

Duty to Supervise

The concept of a counselor's duty and the measure of care required of him or her should also be explored within the framework of traditional school law, particularly dealing with student supervision. More so with counselors than with other school personnel, the duty to supervise frequently involves students with "special needs," whether they be emotionally disturbed, under the influence of drugs or alcohol, or otherwise incapacitated. Once such conditions are made known, or become obvious, the counselor must exercise greater care and supervision than might generally be due. If an incapacitated or disturbed student is under the control or supervision of a counselor, the counselor should be careful not to let the student go his or her own way without making some provision for the student's safety. Such arrangements should be commensurate with the degree of the student's incapacity. According to Professor Seitz (1964):

> If a teacher or administrator contemplates sending a young child home during school hours, she should, as a reasonable prudent person reflect upon whether she is exposing the child to dangers to which the child would not be exposed if it were dismissed at the normal hour. For instance, if the child would be exposed to a very dangerous crossing when no patrol help was on duty and it was injured, it would place the teacher in a precarious position as respects liability.[12]

The test to be applied to the counselor is thus what any reasonably prudent person would do to protect a person who, because of conditions beyond his or her control, is exposed to unusual dangers. This includes the knowledge that the student is incapacitated or disturbed, as well.

Responsibility for Improvement

Generally speaking, courts will not find counselors negligent merely because the client fails to improve during the counseling relationship or if the approach the counselor chooses proves to be erroneous. Courts have ruled that no presumption of negligence arises from a mere mistake in judgment, if that mistake is the type that could be made by the most careful and skilled practitioner of the counseling art. Again, however, the counselor will be judged according to standards applicable to the counseling profession in his or her area.[13]

Only under rare circumstances, if ever, can a counselor give and be held to an assurance of improvement. Basically, the counselor pursues a course dictated by the ethics and standards of the profession. This has been recognized in cases dealing with psychiatric treatment. For example, in *Johnston v. Rodis* (1958), the court held that a physician's statement that he could cure a disease could seldom, if ever, be regarded as a warranty. There is every reason to believe this rule would apply to a counselor who, in the absence of some ill motive, advises a particular course of action that is later found not to have worked. No clear guidelines exist in this area, even in the field of psychiatry, and no appellate courts have ruled in cases involving alleged malpractice arising from such assurances.[14]

When a counselor determines that a course of therapy or treatment is not effective for the client, or if the problems presented are beyond the competence of the counselor, there is a clear professional, ethical duty to terminate the counseling relationship or to seek consultation (standards B.11 and B.12). Although no courts have yet imposed it, there may be a corresponding legal duty to refer or consult when the counselor is not competent to meet the client's needs.[15] At this point, it would seem that a client could sustain a cause of action for malpractice only if he or she could make a case that improvement, of which there was a substantial likelihood, was prevented because the counselor breached the duty to refer the client or consult with another professional concerning treatment. This would be exceptionally difficult to prove, but in at least one case involving a physician who failed to refer a patient with Graves disease to a specialist, liability was found.[16]

Group Counseling

Group therapy has developed into a widely accepted means of treatment for a variety of counseling needs. It is believed that patients learn to understand and communicate more effectively with peers, and that they are better able to put their anxieties or fears into perspective than could be achieved through individual counseling. As the use of group counseling expands, however, counselors must be well trained and skillful in their use of this technique, and must face the possibility of legal challenges arising from the group setting. It is not easy to determine the exact dangers the counselor will encounter in the use of group therapy. No case law has been developed in this area as yet, so analogous situations must be probed in an effort to determine the future direction of the law.

As we have already noted in chapter 3, the legal concept of privileged communication generally does not apply in the group setting, except where there has been a statutory exception. Consequently, it must be assumed that any member of a group, or the counselor leading a group, could be called to testify in court concerning information that may be revealed during group sessions. As a result, the counselor has the responsibility to inform all group participants of the need for confidentiality, and the absence of legal privilege concerning group discussions.

The counselor's relationship to the clients in a group session is the same as in individual counseling sessions: the rendering of service to another. Should the counselor fail to bring to that relationship the skill and care of a qualified counselor practicing within the expert discipline of the profession, the counselor may be liable for breach of the professional duty to clients. The legal requirement of care in the group relationship is more complicated than for the individual counseling setting, however, for several reasons. First, the counselor may be responsible for forming the group and selecting the members. Once the group is formed, the counselor bears the increased duty of supervising the multiple interactions among the various group members.

Standard B.1 of AACD's *Ethical Standards* (1988) (Appendix A) points out that a counselor's primary obligation is always "to respect the integrity and promote the welfare" of clients. But, "in the group setting, the [counselor] is also responsible for taking reasonable precautions to protect individuals from physical and/or psychological trauma resulting from interaction with the group." The *Ethical Guidelines for Group Counselors* (1989)[17] (see Appendix B), provide further guidance in this area and admonish counselors ". . . to give considerable attention to the intent and context of their actions because the attempts of counselors to influence human behavior through group work always have ethical implications" (Preamble). We would add that group work carries additional legal obligations as well.

Counselors must constantly evaluate the size of the group, its appropriateness for each particular member, whether to refer individual members of the group for special help, and whether to bring in an additional counseling professional to assist in the group sessions. Counselors must also be alert to unanticipated encounters within a group, and be prepared to handle potentially explosive situations with a high degree of professional skill to protect each individual group member. This requires extensive training and preparation to avoid potential liability for negligence.

The *Ethical Guidelines for Group Counselors* provide an excellent discussion of the responsibilities of the counselor in group work, both in terms of providing adequate information to clients and in providing group counseling services. The guidelines stress the need to prepare clients adequately before they enter the group so they are fully informed, screening members before they are admitted to a group, setting a norm of confidentiality among group members, protecting group clients from undue pressure or coercion, treating each member of a group individually and equally, and proper follow-up for group members who choose to leave the group prematurely. The guidelines also emphasize the need for adequate professional preparation prior to the use of group therapy, as well as ongoing assessment of the group experience. Because a court may take such professional standards into account when judging whether the actions of a group counselor have been negligent, counselors should become familiar with these guidelines and make every effort to provide services accordingly.

One additional note of caution should be sounded here. As in all counseling situations, the group counselor has the obligation to remain objective and use good professional judgment with all group members. It may be difficult to abide by these dictates with some group members from time to time. Consider the experience of one experienced group leader who became so angry with a group member after repeated personal and physical attacks that he felt compelled to return the attack physically. Recognizing that these feelings violated his professional responsibility to the group as well as to the disruptive client, the counselor immediately sought the help of a professional colleague to deal with his own anger and frustration. A less experienced counselor may not have acted so responsibly, and a malpractice action could have resulted.

Crisis Intervention

Crisis intervention, or crisis management, as a counseling technique is unique and, of course, generally arises out of an emergency situation. The person needing assistance may be only a short step from death or serious injury, and the counselor serves merely as a buffer, hoping to avert tragedy or hold off self-destructive acts or impulses until appropriate medical or psychiatric treatment can be provided.

In a crisis intervention situation the counselor generally has no real control over the person seeking help. Like the Dutch boy who saved his village with a finger in the dike, the counselor serves as a rescuer, attempting to ward off disaster until help arrives. It would be difficult to blame either boy or counselor if the hole should prove too large to block effectively with the plug one has in hand. The general legal principle that applies to rescuers is this: A person is responsible for harm to another *only if the failure to exercise reasonable care increases the risk of harm to another.*[18] The counselor offers to listen to the distressed person, provides words of encouragement or suggestions, and has a duty to use his or her training and skill to assist the distressed individual until therapy or medical treatment can be provided. This does not mean that a counselor is responsible for knowing the history or problems of the person being counseled that are not revealed during the crisis intervention. Consequently, the counselor will be subject to a negligence suit *only if* the counselor fails to use reasonable care in counseling *and* that failure increases the risk of harm to the person. Even if the counselor did not use reasonable care, the counselor will not be held liable for negligence unless that failure *also* increased the risk of harm or left the person in a worse position than before.

It should be noted that we have not used the term "client" to describe the person being counseled in crisis intervention because that denotes the existence of a relationship between the crisis intervention counselor and the individual in need of assistance. If such a relationship exists, the counselor may be held to the same standard of care described previously for the counselor-client relationship. So, for example, consider a counselor who works on a crisis intervention hot line one night each week. One evening he takes a call from someone by whose voice and difficulties he recognizes as a client. In that situation the counselor may have a greater duty to warn family members or provide immediate assistance because the preexisting professional relationship would be presumed to have provided the counselor with sufficient knowledge to render real assistance.

MALPRACTICE IN PARTICULAR SITUATIONS

Birth Control and Abortion Counseling

Most counselors who work with minors will be confronted with requests for information and advice concerning birth control and abortions at some point in their careers. Counselors employed by state welfare and family planning agencies certainly deal with such requests on a daily basis. In fact, many state welfare systems include funds for dissemination of birth control information to their clients. We know that tens of millions of people in this country have used contraceptives for scores of years. In addition to this obvious public acceptance of the practice of birth control, sex and family life education classes are now mandated in many state school systems. Many local jurisdictions have established adolescent health clinics that are empowered to dispense birth control and family planning information to minors who seek their services. Furthermore, in the aftermath of the AIDS epidemic, public service announcements on radio, television, and in magazines openly discuss the use of condoms and advocate "safe sex." Minor children are confronted with these messages on a daily basis.

Unfortunately, despite the widespread availability of this information, many students fail to take advantage of the services, or to use the information effectively. The resulting pregnancies take their toll on health education and social services, and particularly on the emotional and psychological well-being of the teenagers who become pregnant. More than one million teenagers become pregnant in the United States each year, and approximately 42% decide not to have their babies. One small school system in an urban community recently reported over 150 pregnancies in 1989 among its total K-12 population of about 9,000 students. It is apparent that counselors will continue to field queries concerning contraceptives and abortions in the foreseeable future, so it is important to understand the appropriate boundaries of assistance that may be given.

Counselors are generally free to inform clients of the availability of birth control methods without fear of legal liability and to refer clients to family planning or health clinics for more information. Courts have generally struck down, as unconstitutional, statutes that impose criminal penalties on those who disseminate birth control information. For example, Title X of the Public Health Service Act (42 U.S.C. §§300-300a-8) provides for federal funding of family planning services. Under the regulations for that statute, such agencies are required to notify parents of an unemancipated minor within 10 days of dispensing prescription contraceptives to the child.[19] This section of the regulations was struck down in *Planned Parenthood Federation v. Heckler* (1983).[20] Counselors are advised to encourage family involvement in such counseling, but to require notification of parents impinges on the confidentiality rights of minors, according to the court.[21] Other sections of the regulations under Title X have been upheld in court, particularly the nondiscrimination provision.[22] In *Planned Parenthood Association v. Schweiker* (1983), the court ruled that minors could not be discriminated against on the basis of their age in the provision of family planning services.[23] In a few states, however, counselors might still be held accountable for providing such information to minors without the consent of their parents. The Utah Supreme Court, for example, ruled in *Doe v. Planned Parenthood Association of Utah* (1973)[24] that parental consent was a prerequisite to providing birth control information and devices to minors because the prime responsibility for the moral direction of children rests with the parents. The court said that others may not interfere or su-

33

perimpose their standards on minor children without the consent of parents. Consequently, birth control for adolescents remains a highly emotional issue in many communities, and parental consent may still be the preferred avenue in some jurisdictions.

Referral to a health clinic or physician is always appropriate when minors request contraceptive or abortion information or advice. If the counselor decides to provide birth control information, it must be both accurate and complete, and it is important that the client fully understand the information given. Some school boards prescribe that information concerning abstinence also be provided, so it is important that counselors be informed of local rules and statutes in this area.

Advising minor children concerning contraceptives is to be distinguished from counseling such clients about abortions, particularly where the client is already pregnant. Counselors must be cautious not to impose their own views on clients in this highly emotional area. To counsel effectively, they must be aware of the current state of the law concerning abortion and exercise great care to provide accurate information to clients. A brief look at recent opinions of the United States Supreme Court is necessary to understand current federal law relating to abortions.

In 1973 the Supreme Court legalized abortions under certain conditions in its landmark decision in *Roe v. Wade*.[25] Before that decision most states prohibited abortion by law, except where necessary to save the life or health of the mother. Grounded in the Fourteenth Amendment's concept of personal liberty, the Court found that the right to privacy ". . . is broad enough to encompass a woman's decision whether or not to terminate her pregnancy."[26] The Court also established a trimester test for determining the permissible parameters of a woman's right to terminate her pregnancy.

In 1976, the Court struck down portions of a Missouri statute restricting abortions in *Planned Parenthood Association of Central Missouri v. Danforth*.[27] In that case the Supreme Court ruled that a blanket provision in the law requiring parental consent to perform an abortion on a unmarried minor during the first 12 weeks of pregnancy is unconstitutional. According to the Court, the state had no significant interest in restricting such procedures, which should instead be left to the judgment of the attending physician.

That same year, however, the Court upheld the Massachusetts abortion statute, which also required parental consent prior to performing an abortion on an unmarried minor (*Bellotti v. Baird*, 1976).[28] Such statutes pass constitutional muster, according to the Court, if they permit a minor who is capable of giving informed consent to obtain a court order without parental consultation where the court is convinced it is in her best interest. The Supreme Court also upheld a Utah statute requiring a physician to "notify if possible" the parents or guardian or a minor patient prior to performing an abortion (*H. L. v. Matheson*, 1981).[29]

In a second challenge to Missouri's abortion statute in 1983, the Supreme Court again struck down portions of the law, but this time upheld the revised parental consent clause (*Planned Parenthood Association v. Ashcroft*).[30] As revised, the statute allows a pregnant minor to go to juvenile court to obtain permission to have an abortion despite parental disapproval. Because the provision does not allow the juvenile court to deny such a petition unless it first finds the minor not mature enough to make her own decision, the Court ruled that this meets the constitutional requirements. Another 1983 decision, this time challenging Akron, Ohio's, abortion ordinance, sets out several aspects of the constitutional requirements on the issue (*Akron v. Akron Center for Reproductive Health, Inc.*).[31] Extensive portions of the Court's opinion in this case are included in Appendix D to provide counselors with a summary of the Court's position until 1989.

The Supreme Court reconsidered the abortion issue in 1989 in *Webster v. Reproductive Health Services*,[32] but did not specifically overrule *Roe v. Wade*, when it upheld a Missouri statute restricting the availability of publicly funded abortion services. The Missouri statute also requires physicians to test for fetal viability at 20 weeks, two thirds of the way through the second trimester of a pregnancy. Furthermore, the preamble of the Missouri statute expressed the intention of stopping abortions. According to the Court, the language in the preamble did not bind anyone, and the public funding of abortions was never constitutionally protected anyway, so upholding the Missouri statute had no affect on *Roe v. Wade*'s constitutional issues.

There were several opinions in *Webster* that addressed the constitutional question of whether the state can prohibit abortions, yet only Justice Scalia wrote that he would overturn *Roe* altogether. The other Justices still uphold a woman's constitutional right to privacy and to control her pregnancy as set out in *Roe v. Wade*, although there is some indication that the pragmatic trimester test might be discarded in favor of a fetal viability test in future decisions.

The *Webster* decision highlighted, however, that states do have the right to regulate abortions under *Roe v. Wade*, and will continue to do so. In the wake of the decision, the Pennsylvania General Assembly passed a sweeping reform of its abortion statute.[33] The Pennsylvania law permits abortions based on a physician's "best clinical judgment . . . in light of all factors . . . relevant to the well-being of the woman," up to 24 weeks gestational age, and thereafter only under certain circumstances. The law requires informed consent prior to the procedure and specifies the content of the information to be provided. It also requires parental consent prior to performing the procedure on a minor, but requires prompt judicial determination on petitions to conduct an abortion without parental consent. Spousal notification is also generally required, except in limited situations. Finally, the law specifically prohibits abortions based solely on the sex of the fetus.

Another aspect of this question concerns the "judicial bypass" around parental notification and consent when a minor seeks an abortion. In the past, the Court has upheld state statutes that require parental notification and consent so long as, like the Pennsylvania statute, there is a judicial avenue for a teenager to secure an abortion when it is not in the best interest of the teenager to inform her parents. During the 1989–1990 term the Court has been asked to consider two cases involving states' attempts to eliminate this "bypass" from a law, and whether it is necessary to inform both parents, even a divorced or abusive parent. The question may also arise whether teenagers have the same constitutionally protected right to privacy in the context of the abortion decision as do adults.

Three particular concepts are important to counselors. First, the right to an abortion is guaranteed by the United States Constitution. States may regulate the performance of abortions, however, to protect the health and safety of their citizens (presently a trimester test, restricting abortions during the third trimester except where the life or health of the mother is in jeopardy). Furthermore, states are not obligated to provide public funding for abortions.

Second, the Court has ruled that parents of an unmarried pregnant minor have some rights to know about and consent to an abortion. But there must be some means by which a minor can prove her maturity, demonstrate informed consent to the procedure, and, despite parental objection, obtain a court order permitting an abortion.

Finally, physicians are the proper persons to advise pregnant women on the abortion procedure and assist in their decision making. Such duties can be delegated to other individuals either supervised by the physician or "specially trained to provide all the information needed and counsel the pregnant client" under the *Akron* decision. That case clearly recognized the role counselors play in ensuring a woman's informed consent, but emphasized that they must have the necessary training to enable them to counsel their clients effectively, be they minors or adults. Furthermore, states may establish minimum qualifications for such counselors.[34] This is consistent with standard B.12 of the AACD *Ethical Standards* (1988), which directs a counselor to avoid or terminate a counseling relationship if the counselor determines he or she is unable to be of professional assistance to the client. In the case of a pregnant client seeking abortion advice, a knowledgeable referral would be prudent.

Prescribing or Administering Drugs or Treatment

Although it is sometimes difficult to apply general principles of law to a specific situation, in no area of law is it easier than in the prescription or administration of drugs. The federal government and all states, recognizing the potentially dangerous character of all drugs, have established statutes restricting the prescription or administration of drugs to individuals in the medical field who are specially trained to do a proper job. In fact, anyone who is not a licensed physician or psychiatrist who prescribes or administers controlled substances is, in reality, practicing medicine without a license.

As has been seen in previous negligence cases, counselors or other professionals are held to the duty of reasonable care or skill in their vocation. Under that standard, a counselor is protected in his or her professional capacity, even if mistaken in judgment, so long as the counselor exercises reasonable care. Where the counselor steps out of the counseling field into the field of medicine, however, the counselor will be judged by the more rigorous standards of the medical profession. Accordingly, a counselor who provides medical services to a client is not using due care if he or she is not trained and licensed to administer the treatment that is reasonable and proper under the circumstances. Even in a emergency situation, counselors should never recommend or administer drugs, and one who does so cannot always rely on the Good Samaritan laws for protection. A first aid specialist, nurse, or emergency squad should be summoned if emergency treatment is necessary.

Sexual Misconduct

Standard B.14 of the AACD *Ethical Standards* clearly establishes that "sexual relationships with clients are unethical" and admonishes members to "avoid any type of sexual intimacies with clients." Despite considerable publicity in recent years, many clients still do not know that sexual relationships between clients and counselors are unethical and, in some states, illegal. Clients who have been victims of such relationships clearly have the choice of filing ethical, administrative, or legal complaints against their former counselors, and this process has been recognized as a positive and healing experience for some clients.[35] Furthermore, lawsuits based on sexual misconduct are becoming more common and may be financially rewarding to certain clients. The terms of many malpractice insurance policies now routinely exclude coverage for sexual misconduct, limit the damages that will be paid, or pay only for the legal defense of the counselor, but not for any damages that may be awarded.

Generally, clients alleging sexual misconduct must prove in court that there was sexual contact between the counselor and the client, that the client suffered some emotional injury as a result of the contact, and in some states, that the contact occurred under the guise of treatment. In several states, however, a sexual relationship between a counselor and a client is sufficient grounds for a claim of negligence, whether it occurred under the guise of treatment or not. It is also possible that the spouse or companion of a client who has engaged in sexual relations with a counselor may bring a malpractice action and recover actual damages.[36] Counselors should also be aware that there may be criminal penalties for engaging in sexual relations with clients, as described in chapter 5.

Other Civil Actions

Illegal Search and Seizure

Potential civil liability for illegal search and seizure usually arises only in the school setting and will generally affect only school counselors. Particularly as counselors become more involved with disciplinary proceedings in schools, they are increasingly required to search either the person of a student, or his or her locker or dormitory room. In so doing, the counselor risks invading the student's constitutionally protected rights to privacy and to freedom from unreasonable search and seizure as set forth in the Fourth Amendment. The Fourth Amendment applies to federal and state government officials and is enforced by means of the exclusionary rule, whereby evidence obtained as the result of an illegal search may not be used as evidence in a court of law (*Mapp v. Ohio*, 1961).[37] If a counselor is asked to assist the police in conducting a search, either with or without a warrant, the counselor may follow reasonable orders free from fear of future legal action. The counselor in this setting is functioning only at the request of duly constituted authorities and presumably has not initiated the search.

Individuals' privacy rights also are guaranteed by the Constitution, and any "illegal search by a private individual is a trespass in violation of the right of privacy. . . . Any intentional invasion of, or interference with property, property rights, personal rights or personal liberties causing injury without just cause or excuse is an actionable tort" (*Sutherland v. Kroger Co.*, 1959).[38] As a general rule, teachers or counselors have always been considered "private persons" in the jargon of search and seizure. The only "professional" recognized under the law was the law enforcement officer. Like any other private person, the counselor is not liable for an alleged illegal search of a pupil so long as the counselor acted with reasonable judgment, and was motivated by reasonable cause, without malice, and for the good of the pupil. Thus, counselors were generally excluded from coverage of the Fourth Amendment's proscriptions, but could be sued in tort for invasion of privacy unless these criteria were met.

In *New Jersey v. T.L.O.* (1985)[39], however, the Supreme Court ruled that public school officials, including counselors, are instrumentalities of the state and are subject to the Fourth Amendment commands. As the Court wrote,

> In carrying out searches and other disciplinary functions pursuant to such policies, school officials act as representatives of the State, not merely as surrogates for the parents, and they cannot claim the parents' immunity from the strictures of the Fourth Amendment.

Despite the fact that counselors and other public school administrators are "representatives of the state" and are therefore bound by the parameters of the Fourth Amendment, this does not mean that all searches are improper. Courts use a balancing of interests test to determine whether a search is "reasonable" according to the facts presented. As one court concluded, although a student "has a constitutional interest in freedom from governmental intrusion into his privacy . . . the State has an interest in educating children and to do so it is necessary to maintain order in and around the classroom" (*Interest of L.L.*, 1979).[40]

The Supreme Court gave school officials broad powers to search students suspected of carrying weapons, dealing drugs, or violating other laws or school rules in the *New Jersey* case. The opinion adopts the position that the Fourth Amendment's prohibition on unreasonable searches and seizures applies to searches conducted by public school officials, as well as by law enforcement officers. Furthermore, students have legitimate expectations of privacy. But the Court also recognized that schools have an equally legitimate need to maintain a learning environment for all students. In order to meet this latter need, the Court ruled that the legality of a student search "should depend simply on the reasonableness, under all the circumstances, of the search." Whether a search is reasonable will depend on whether

> ... there are reasonable grounds for suspecting that the search will turn up evidence that the student has violated or is violating either the law or the rules of the school. Such a search will be permissible in its scope when the measures adopted are reasonably related to the objectives of the search and not excessively intrusive in light of the age and sex of the student and the nature of the infraction. (*New Jersey v. T.L.O.*, 1985[41])

As demonstrated by the case law, school authorities, including counselors, stand in a unique position when it comes to searching school premises. Search warrants are unnecessary to access a student's locker or dormitory room so long as the official has "reasonable suspicion to believe" that illegal substances or items capable of undermining the order and good health of the school environment may be concealed there. Counselors are advised to avoid searches of students to the extent possible, but where this is not possible, counselors must be guided by a standard of reasonableness, as determined by all the facts of the case.

It should be noted that the policy of a public high school requiring all members of the band to submit to a search of their luggage prior to embarking on a concert trip was ruled unconstitutional by the Supreme Court of Washington. Although the court recognized a statistical probability that some contraband would be found, the school officials lacked any reasonable belief that drugs or alcohol were hidden in the students' luggage (*Kuehn v. Renton School District No. 403*, 1985).[42]

Defamation

Another source of potential civil liability for counselors is found in the tort action called "defamation." Defamation embodies the important public policy that each person should be free to enjoy his or her reputation unimpaired by false or defamatory attacks, except in certain cases where a paramount public interest dictates that individuals be free to write or speak without fear of civil liability. Violations of this right form the basis for the action, which turns on whether the communication or publication tends, or is reasonably calculated, to cause harm to the reputation of another.[43] At common law, defamation was broken down into two separate actions: *slander*, a spoken or uttered word that defames a person, and *libel*, which is a defamatory writing. For most purposes today the two forms are treated as one action.

Although there have been major changes in the law of defamation in recent years, for the purposes of most counselors the law is fairly clear. The key elements of a defamation suit brought by a private person are as follows:

> (1) the information must be defamatory, that is the party must be exposed to hatred, ridicule, contempt, or pecuniary loss; (2) the de-

famatory information must have been communicated to another person other than the person defamed by the information; (3) the party defamed must be a living person; and (4) the person defamed must have suffered some type of injury or loss. (Lovett, 1980, p. 4)[44]

In addition to obvious injuries such as loss of a job, honor, or an award, damages in such a suit may also be based on mental suffering and loss of reputation. Some states also continue to recognize the common law action for slander, in which a person could be held liable for any communication that (a) imputes to another the commission of a serious crime, (b) imputes that another has some loathsome disease, (c) imputes that a woman is unchaste, or (d) adversely affects a person's business, trade, or profession.

The primary areas in which counselors are exposed to liability for defamation are in the publication of records, in letters of reference or recommendation, and in "loose talk" that may be untrue or damaging to the client as revealed to a third party. Consequently, counselors must be aware of the limitations that must be placed on written or verbal statements concerning clients. If the client can be identified from the information provided in a conversation or writing, even though the name is carefully withheld, the counselor may become the uncomfortable subject of a lawsuit claiming damages as the result of that indiscretion.

The major defense to a defamation action is the truth of the statement or information communicated to a third party. In many states this is an absolute defense to the action, just as at common law, although some states also require the statement to have been in good faith and for a legitimate purpose. Counselors who make truthful statements about clients without some legitimate purpose, or based on rumors, could find themselves subject to a defamation suit just as for any other gossip.

If truth were the only defense to a defamation action, counselors would find themselves subjected to frequent lawsuits. The law recognizes that in many situations the interests of the immediate participants or of society at large dictate that bona fide communication to others should not be hamstrung by the fear of lawsuits.[45] In these cases, the law has created "privileges" to allow counselors and others to make communications that, except for the particular occasion or circumstances under which they were made, would be defamatory and actionable. In other words, in certain cases society has a greater interest in free communication than an individual has in his or her concern for personal reputation.[46] Such privileges are granted by statute in almost all states for the proper discharge of official duties, and are to be distinguished from the privileged communications discussed in chapter 3 concerning confidentiality. In that discussion, privilege is analyzed as protection from revealing client confidences should a counselor be called to testify in a court of law. This is a right that belongs solely to the client and binds the counselor to silence. When the term "privilege" is used in connection with defamation actions it describes a privilege *to communicate*, which protects the counselor against money-damage defamation suits. The two privileges are not analogous.

When privilege is discussed in connection with defamation there are two types of protected communication: that which is *absolutely* privileged and that which is *qualifiedly* privileged. Absolute privilege is based on the concept that the public interest in unimpeded communication in certain cases completely outweighs society's concern for an individual's reputation. It is the occasion or circumstance under which the communication is made that is privileged, and absolute privilege is designed not to protect the public servant, but to promote public welfare. Thus members of the legislature, judges, jurors, lawyers, and witnesses may speak freely in the exercise of their respective functions without fear of prosecution.[47]

Qualified privilege exists in situations in which society's interest in unhampered communication is *conditionally limited* by the general mores as to what is fair and reasonable according to the practical necessities of daily life. Stated another way, certain individuals have a right to receive confidential reports or information based on their positions that is not appropriate for publication to society at large. Generally, any statement made in a reasonable manner by one who is carrying out duties for a legitimate purpose will be protected by the qualified privilege. Counselors are frequently called upon in the course of their professional duties to make statements concerning clients to other people who have a corresponding duty or interest in receiving that information. For example, it might be necessary to inform a colleague, or a parent, that a client's difficulties stem from the use of illegal drugs. A prospective employer may request general information about a client or seek specific information concerning ability or character.[48] Counselors may need to notify a social service agency of problems in a family to ensure the safety of a client.[49] So long as such communications are made in good faith, expressing the facts as known to the counselor, and are published only to those who have a proper interest in receiving the information, they will be protected. However, if the information is published improperly or excessively (through gossip, for example), or if the communication is maliciously motivated, the privilege could be lost and a court could find liability.

Juries are commonly instructed to review five elements of communications to determine whether a communication is qualifiedly privileged. They are:

- The communication must be made in good faith.
- It must promote an acceptable interest.
- The statement is limited in scope to this purpose.
- The occasions for transmittal must be proper.
- Publication must be in a proper manner, and only to proper parties.[50]

If all five conditions prevail, the communication will be considered privileged, and even a false statement will not be actionable in a defamation suit.

If the statement is published excessively or with malice, however, the privilege will be lost. Malice is defined legally as bad faith or action taken because of an unacceptable motive. Many jurisdictions hold that malice in the moral sense (hate, vindictiveness, animosity) need not be shown to forfeit the privilege. It is sufficient to show that a communication was made "without just cause or excuse" that is in "reckless disregard of the rights of others."[51] Using this standard, a court would consider whether the counselor had exercised sufficient care in ascertaining the truth of the information passed on to a third party.

For example, in a libel action brought because a credit information company had inadvertently disseminated false financial information to subscribers and did not attempt to correct it, the jury awarded the plaintiff damages for injury to his reputation. Because reporting credit information to subscribers creates a conditional privilege, it would be necessary for the plaintiff to show that the credit company's actions were the result of malice. The court held that the negligence or carelessness of the credit company constituted malice because its conduct amounted to conscious indifference and reckless disregard of the rights of the plaintiff. Counselors must also be cautious about client information disclosed to others. If false information is ever transmitted to a third party, corrections should be made as soon as possible.

Counselors who act in a professional manner and are cautious about client information communicated to third parties will generally be protected from defamation actions by the qualified privilege. Here again, the AACD *Ethical Standards* provide excellent guidance for professional counselors in the disclosure of client information.

Invasion of Privacy

Despite the truthfulness of a defamatory statement and the qualified immunity granted in the counseling situation, a counselor may still be held liable in an action for invasion of privacy if derogatory information is communicated to a third party who has no need or privilege to receive it. The action is based upon undue interference in the affairs of an individual through exposure or communication of his or her private affairs. The injury may result from truthful, but damaging, publications, and the person bringing the suit need not prove that he or she has suffered any special injuries. During the 1960s and 1970s the dangers and injustices caused by the compilation and dissemination of data and files on the personal and business affairs of millions of Americans were exposed. There are numerous stories of both serious outrages and humorous foul-ups caused by erroneous material in various data and credit department computers. Unfortunately, trivial or erroneous material can haunt and harm individuals throughout their lives.

The problem is no less severe in the context of educational records and testing. Several court cases have addressed these concerns over the years and established a "balancing test" to weigh the invasion of an individual's privacy against the public interest in the information. In *Merriken v. Cressman* (1973), for example, a school district proposed to use a testing program to identify potential drug abusers among its eighth grade students. The court found that the public's interest in trying to prevent drug abuse through this means was outweighed by the potential harm to the students from lack of informed parental consent and lack of strict confidentiality of the results. The court concluded as a matter of law that the testing program violated the right of the students and parents to privacy, a right guaranteed by the Bill of Rights.[52]

The Congress acted to correct such situations in the educational arena through passage of the Education Amendments of 1974, which contained the "Protection of the Rights and Privacy of Parents and Students Amendment," otherwise known as the Buckley Amendment[53], discussed in chapter 3. In introducing the bill, Senator Buckley (R-NY) stated:

> Many schools do not ask parents' permission to give personality or psychiatric tests to their children, or to obtain data from the children on their parents or family life. Some of these tests include questions dealing with the most personal feelings and habits of children and their families. Some of these data, in personally identifiable form, [are] given to other government agencies or to private organizations. Some of it ends up on Federal computers in the caverns of the Department of Health, Education and Welfare . . .[54]

Counselors working in educational institutions should be thoroughly familiar with the text of the Buckley Amendment and the student rights and consent requirements specified in the regulations that accompany it.[55]

Counselors employed in all fields are subject to potential liability for invasion of privacy if they administer tests without first fully informing the client of (1) the criteria to be used, (2) what skills or factors the test is designed to measure, (3) the possible uses of test results, or (4) if they fail to explain the test results. In response to the consumer movement, for example, New York and other states have enacted legislation requiring testing agencies to provide various notices to test subjects and to disclose fully the factors outlined above.[56] Counselors should keep these criteria in mind when conducting testing and protect the written records of that testing.

It is also important to note that although most educational research and testing, public surveys, and observations of public behavior are specifically excluded from the U.S. Department of Health and Human Service's regulations concerning research on human subjects, the full force of the regulations may be held to apply in some cases where test responses are recorded in such a manner that the identities of the subjects can be discovered. This shows the degree to which that department believes subjects are entitled to privacy.[57]

The confidentiality of records also poses a problem for counselors because of concerns about the invasion of privacy. The questions as to what should be included in a student or client record, and who might have access to that record, can generally be answered by the rules concerning defamation. First, reasonable care must be taken to ensure that the contents of the record are

43

accurate. Any counselor who makes an entry designed to unfairly injure the client would run a serious risk of a lawsuit, even if the information were true. As the court in *A.B.C. Needlecraft Co. v. Dun & Bradstreet, Inc.* (1957) concluded, the malice necessary to destroy a qualified privilege can consist of such reckless disregard of the rights of another as to constitute the equivalent of ill will.[58] Entering misleading or false information, or failing to make adequate corrections of such information could meet this lower threshold definition of malice.

Second, the contents of records should be made known only to those who have a legitimate interest in them (for example, parents, professional colleagues, prospective employers) as defined by statute, regulation, or as established by a written release of information signed by the client or a parent. These general rules are, of course, subject to more specific regulations or laws that may govern records in a particular state institution, agency, or school system. Counselors will not generally be held liable in a suit for invasion of privacy if required by law to disclose information, or if the disclosure was not malicious, and was made to serve certain overriding competing public interests, such as health regulations or (in the wake of the *Tarasoff* decision) protecting a potential victim.

Breach of Contract

Another area of potential liability for counselors is contract law. Contracts may be created in two forms: express contracts and implied contracts. Most people are familiar with the express contract. Usually written documents, express contracts are signed by the parties and spell out the understanding as to the rights and responsibilities of each. Express contracts made orally are just as binding on the parties, although proving the terms of the agreement at some later time may be difficult.

Implied contracts arise either through the relationship of the parties or as a result of actions of the parties that create a contractual relationship. For example, a counselor may expressly or implicitly promise certain results or benefits of counseling to a client. The counselor may agree to provide treatment for a certain number of sessions, at a set time, or for a set fee. All these aspects of the relationship form the basis of the contract with the client, and may give rise to an implied contract. If the counselor, absent some justification, fails to uphold his or her end of the bargain under the contract, the counselor can be held liable for the breach of the contract in a suit by the client. The counselor may be held liable for any damages suffered by the client as a result of the breach, including direct, incidental, and consequential damages (Lovett, 1980, n.1).[59]

Other considerations may be viewed as terms of the counselor-client contract as well. For example, one commentator suggested that public knowledge of the ethical standards of the medical profession and the secrecy provisions of the Hippocratic oath would be sufficient to justify a patient's belief that a physician must keep patient information confidential. Consequently, disclosure of such information might be treated as a breach of one of the terms of an implied contract between a physician and patient.[60] To extrapolate from this theory, a counselor could be held liable for breach of an implied contract with a client for disclosure of confidential information to others, in addition to tort liability for invasion of privacy or defamation.

Courts may also view professional advertising as terms of an express or implied contract with clients. For example, a firm including such terms as *licensed, bonded, certified*, or the like in directory advertising will be held to fulfill those terms, or be found in breach of contract. Along this same line, deceptive or misleading advertising may simultaneously give rise to an action for violation of state deceptive or fraudulent advertising statutes.

Counselors should exercise care in all aspects of a client relationship, of course. Special attention should clearly be given to items that may form the basis of any contract with a client, whether express or implied. To protect themselves, counselors may benefit from written agreements detailing such items as the number and timing of sessions, fees, and payment terms. A counselor should never contract with a client concerning specific results or outcome of treatment, however, which may prove impossible to achieve.

Copyright Infringement

As we have mentioned previously, the widespread use of microcomputers has proved of immeasurable benefit to counselors and administrators worldwide in recent years. Many agencies and institutions now commonly preserve counseling records and data on computer data bases and use computers to facilitate client assessment and research. With the efficiency of this wonderful tool, however, a host of concerns have developed of which counselors should be aware. Many of these are addressed in the 1988 revision of the AACD *Ethical Standards* and relate to the potential misuse of information; confidentiality; client misconceptions; counselor training; accuracy of computer-based programs; and the validity of test interpretations, to name a few. Certainly other ethical areas wait to be addressed in this area as well.

Another important consideration for counselors who use computers in record keeping and testing is the application of federal copyright laws and licensing agreements. Most adults are aware of the general proscriptions on plagiarism and the protection for written and creative works offered by copyright laws. Such protections also extend to testing materials, scoring keys, normative tables, and report forms, however, and to other computer software applications, according to the 8th Circuit Court of Appeals. In *Regents of University of Minnesota v. Applied Innovations, Inc.* (1989)[61] the court ruled that the development, reproduction, marketing, and distribution of software for scoring the Minnesota Multiphasic Personality Inventory (MMPI) infringed on the University of Minnesota's copright of the test because it included copyrighted portions of the instrument. Obviously, not all counselors are engaged in the development of such scoring software, but this proscription applies to *users* of such programs as well.

According to a recent article in the AACD *Guidepost*, "Bootlegged computer programs pose a serious threat to the rights of copyright holders and to the integrity of testing itself."[62] It was also pointed out that the use of bootlegged programs deprives test creators of revenue to which they are entitled and, perhaps more importantly, could lead to the promulgation of defective products that could adversely affect client treatment. Counselors are cautioned to comply with copyright laws and licensing agreements when they purchase computer software just as they exercise care to comply with copyright laws in written or other materials.

References

1. Robinson, S. E., & Gross, D. R. (1986). Ethics in mental health counseling. In A. J. Palmo & W. J. Weikel (Eds.), *Foundations of mental health counseling* (pp. 309–327). Springfield, IL: Charles C Thomas.
2. Robinson, S. (1988). Counselor competence and malpractice suits: Opposite sides of the same coin. *Counseling and Human Development, 20*(9), 1–8.
3. Lovett, T. (1980, February). Exploring potential counselor liability in civil, criminal actions. *ASCA Newsletter*, pp. 3–4.
4. *See also* Corey, G., Corey, M. S., & Callahan, P. (1988). *Issues and ethics in the helping profession* (3rd ed.). Pacific Grove, CA: Brooks/Cole.
5. 57 Am.Jur.2d *Negligence* §33.
6. Horak v. Biris, 130 Ill.App.3d 140, 85 Ill.Dec. 599, 474 N.E.2d 13 (1985).
7. Rowe v. Bennett, 514 A.2d 802 (Me.1986).
8. Restatement of Law of Torts, §323 (2d ed.).
9. Bogust v. Iverson, 102 N.W.2d 228 (Wisc. 1960).
10. Tarasoff v. Regents of the University of California, 551 P.2d 334 (Cal.Sup.Ct. 1976).
11. Bellah v. Greenson, 181 Cal.App.3d 614 (1978).
12. Seitz (1964). *Legal responsibility under tort law of school personnel and school districts as regards negligent conduct toward pupils*, 15 Hastings L.J. 495, 505–506.
13. 99 A.L.R.2d 619; 58 A.L.R.4th 977.
14. Johnston v. Rodis, 251 F.2d 917 (D.D.C. 1958) 99 A.L.R.2d 604, 605.
15. 19 A.L.R.2d 1206.
16. Wozniak v. Lifoff, 242 Kan. 583, 750 P.2d 971 (1988). In this case the physician was an inexperienced internist who also prescribed medication to the patient, which the patient subsequently used to kill herself.
17. Association for Specialists in Group Work. *Ethical guidelines for group counselors.* (1989). Alexandria, VA: Author.
18. 57 Am.Jur.2d, *Negligence* §33.
19. 42 C.F.R. §59.5(a)(12).
20. Planned Parenthood Federation v. Heckler, 712 F.2d 650 (D.C.Cir. 1983).
21. *See also* New York v. Heckler, 719 F.2d 1191 (2d Cir. 1983).
22. 42 C.F.R. §59.5(a)(4).
23. Planned Parenthood Association v. Schweiker, 700 F.2d 710 (D.C.Cir. 1983).
24. Doe v. Planned Parenthood Association of Utah, 510 P.2d 75.
25. (Utah 1973). Roe v. Wade, 410 U.S. 113 (1973).
26. 410 U.S., at 153.

27. Planned Parenthood Association of Central Missouri v. Danforth, 428 U.S. 52, 96 S.Ct. 2831, 49 L.Ed.2d 788 (1976).
28. Bellotti v. Baird, 428 U.S. 132, 96 S.Ct. 2857, 49 L.Ed.2d 844 (1976).
29. H. L. v. Matheson, 450 U.S. 398, 101 S.Ct. 1164, 67 L.Ed.2d 388 (1981).
30. Planned Parenthood Association v. Ashcroft, 462 U.S. 476, 103 S.Ct. 2517, 76 L.Ed. 2d 733 (1983).
31. Akron v. Akron Center for Reproductive Health, Inc., 462 U.S. 416, 103 S. Ct. 2481, 76 L.Ed.2d 687 (1983).
32. Webster v. Reproductive Health Services, ___ U.S. ___, 109 S. Ct. 3040, ___ L.Ed.2d ___ (1989).
33. 1989 Pa. Legis. Serv. 657 [Act No.1989–64 amending Pa. Stat. Ann. tit. 18, §§ 3203–4302 (Purdon 1989)].
34. Akron v. Akron Center for Reproductive Health, Inc., *supra*, 76 L.Ed.2d at 714–715.
35. Hotelling, K. (1988). Ethical, legal and administrative options to address sexual relationships between counselor and client. *Journal of Counseling and Development, 67*, 233–237.
36. *See* Horak v. Biris, *supra*, and Rowe v. Bennett, *supra*.
37. Mapp v. Ohio, 367 U.S. 643, 81 S.Ct. 1684, 6 L.Ed.2d 1081 (1961).
38. Sutherland v. Kroger Co., 110 S.E.2d 716 (W.Va. 1959).
39. New Jersey v. T.L.O., 469 U.S. 325, 83 L.Ed.2d 720, 105 S.Ct. 733 (1985).
40. Interest of L.L., 90 Wis.2d 585, 280 N.W.2d 343 (Wis.App. 1979).
41. New Jersey v. T.L.O., *supra*, 469 U.S. at 342.
42. Kuehn v. Renton School District No. 403, 694 P.2d 1078 (Wash. 1985).
43. 50 Am.Jur.2d, *Libel and Slander*, §1.
44. Lovett, T. (1980, February). Exploring potential counselor liability in civil, criminal actions. *ASCA Newsletter*, pp. 3–4.
45. Coleman v. Newark Morning Ledger Co., 149 A.2d 193 (N.J. 1959).
46. 50 Am.Jur.2d, *Libel and Slander* §192.
47. 50 Am.Jur.2d, *Libel and Slander*, §193. *See also* Toker v. Pollak, 376 N.E.2d 163 (N.Y. 1978), and Tiedemann v. Superior Court, 148 Cal.Rptr. 242 (Cal.App. 1978).
48. Brown, R. S. (1987, March). Can you be sued for letters of reference? *Education Digest*, pp. 54–56.
49. Dick v. Watowan County, 551 F. Supp. 983 (D.Minn. 1982).
50. Owens v. Scott Publishing Co., 284 P.2d 296 (Wash. 1955).
51. Dun & Bradstreet v. Robinson, 345 S.W.2d 34 (Ark. 1961).
52. Merriken v. Cressman, 364 F. Supp. 913 (E.D.Pa. 1973).
53. 20 U.S.C. §1232g (1974).
54. Cong.Rec., Vol. 120, No. 65 (May 9, 1964) at p. 7533.
55. Privacy Rights of Parents and Students—Final Regulations, Department of Health, Education and Welfare, 34 C.F.R. §§99.1–99.37.
56. N.Y. Education Law §§ 340–348 (McKinney 1988).
57. 45 C.F.R., Part 46 (1989).
58. A.B.C. Needlecraft Co. v. Dun & Bradstreet, Inc., 245 F.2d 775, 777 (2d Cir. 1957).
59. Lovett, T. (1980), *supra*.
60. 20 A.L.R.3d 1109, 1113; *See also* 79 Harv.L.Rev 1723 (June 1966).
61. Regents of University of Minnesota v. Applied Innovations, Inc., 876 F.2d 626 (8th Cir. 1989).
62. Federal appeals court affirms copyright infringement ruling (August 10, 1989). *AACD Guidepost*, p. 9.

Chapter 5

AVOIDING CRIMINAL LIABILITY

Certainly few counselors ever anticipate that they might become defendants in a criminal action simply by practicing their profession. Fortunately, very few ever do. But counselors should be aware of certain occupational hazards that could lead to criminal liability. The ideal for professional counselors is to maintain a certain distance between themselves and their clients so they may advise the clients in a professional way. Occasionally, however, situations arise that might lead counselors to go much further in protecting their clients, or to provide emotional support and comfort, than the law literally allows. In such cases, the counselor may unwittingly risk criminal liability.

Criminal liability resulting from the professional practice of counseling might result in a variety of criminal charges. We shall discuss four of these charges in this chapter:

- Accessory to a crime;
- Failure to report suspected child abuse;
- Contributing to the delinquency of a minor;
- Sexual misconduct.

ACCESSORY TO A CRIME

Although counselors are honor-bound to protect the integrity and promote the welfare of their clients, they also have an obligation to society at large that may override their duty to the individual client. The law makes it clear that one who advises or encourages the commission of a crime can be charged as an accessory to the crime, even though the person took no active part in its commission. This is called "accessory before the fact," and an individual convicted of such activity faces criminal penalties. The elements of the offense include the following: (a) evidence exists that the defendant in some way contributed to the crime by aiding or advising the alleged perpetrator, (b) the defendant was not present when the crime was committed, and (c) the alleged perpetrator is convicted of the crime or admits to having committed the crime (*State v. Woods*, 1982).[1]

There is precedent that merely concealing knowledge that a felony is to be committed does not, without more, make the party concealing it an ac-

49

cessory before the fact.[2] Thus a counselor who learns during a counseling session that a crime is to be committed may not have to reveal that knowledge to authorities, but counselors should be cautious in this gray area. Particularly in view of the *Tarasoff* decision (see chapter 3), counselors must reach a balance between the confidential communications of a client and the need to preserve the safety and well-being of society. Although there is no hard-and-fast rule to follow, if a counselor believes a client is about to commit a crime that would threaten the safety, health, or well-being of others, or would threaten their property, the counselor has a duty to prevent the act from occurring. This may be an active duty that extends to contacting local law enforcement authorities or the intended victim, or it may be limited to attempting to discourage the client, depending on the circumstances of the case.

One thing should be clear from this discussion: A person need not participate personally in a criminal act to be charged with an offense. Depending on the law of the particular state, if a counselor learns a client is about to steal or destroy property, sell or otherwise deal in drugs,[3] harm or injure another person, or supply information or paraphernalia that would assist someone else in committing a criminal offense, and if the counselor does not take adequate measures to prevent the offense, the counselor can be held criminally liable as an accessory before the fact.

A person who assists or aids a felon *after* a crime has been committed, knowing that the crime has been committed, may be similarly charged as an "accessory after the fact." An accessory after the fact is generally defined as "one who, knowing that a felony has been committed by another, receives, relieves, comforts or assists the felon, or in any manner aids him to escape arrest or punishment."[4] Three elements must be met to render one an accessory after the fact:

1. A felony must have already been committed;
2. The person charged as an accessory must have knowledge that the person he or she is assisting committed the felony; and
3. The accessory must harbor or assist the felon, intending to shield the felon from the law.

Evidence that a person helped to hide a felon, lent the felon money, gave advice, provided goods, offered transportation,[5] blocked the path of pursuers, or gave false information tending to mislead authorities has been held sufficient to sustain a conviction as accessory after the fact.[6] It would be inaccurate, however, to say that *any* affirmative assistance or relief automatically results in charges that one has been an accessory. Even those acts just enumerated have not always been sufficient to justify conviction where there is no evidence that assistance was provided with the intention of "harboring or assisting" the felon.[7]

The law does not distinguish between a friend helping a friend, and business associate assisting another business associate, or, for our purposes, a counselor aiding a client. The criminal prohibition is general in nature, and there is no exemption for counselors under the law. By applying the body of case law to the counseling situation it is clear that a counselor who discovers that a client has committed a crime has the obligation to try to persuade the client to turn him- or herself in to law enforcement authorities, and must refrain from helping the client to hide from the police.

FAILURE TO REPORT SUSPECTED CHILD ABUSE

As discussed in chapter 3, certain communications between counselors and their clients may be considered "privileged"; that is to say, they will be protected from the requirement of disclosure in a court of law in some jurisdictions. In addition to this privilege, it is generally agreed that all communications between a client and counselor should remain confidential. Although this concern for confidentiality is important to the counseling relationship, it has been demonstrated that there are times when the needs of society outweigh the right of an individual to keep communications confidential. One of the clearest examples of this balancing test is in the case of suspected child abuse.[8]

Many state laws now require timely, good faith reporting of cases of suspected child abuse, and the failure to do so may lead to prosecution. Although this primarily affects school counselors, it is imperative that all counselors who work with families and children be aware of the scope of the law in their local jurisdictions. Many school districts have attempted to minimize the potential for improper reports by school counselors by establishing procedures for a team review of cases before reporting.[9] Despite such measures, the area is a difficult one for counselors, and there is real potential for erroneous reports and abuse of the system.

To further confuse the situation, statutes vary widely by state, and authorities disagree over the definition and appropriateness of the standards used to determine emotional abuse, sexual abuse, or neglect.[10] Consequently, it is imperative that counselors clearly understand the scope of the law in their jurisdiction, be alert to possible cases that fit within the statutory definitions of abuse or neglect, make a good faith effort to determine that reports of abuse are factual and accurate, document the case as fully as possible for the record, consult with other appropriate school personnel (principal, teacher, nurse), and keep the best interests of the child in mind when making the report to the child protective services agency.

Counselors can play an important role in establishing written school district procedures for reporting cases of suspected child abuse for staff. Such procedures should be thoroughly reviewed by legal counsel before implementation. They should set out the state statutory and regulatory requirements, a procedural chain of reporting between the person suspecting the abuse and the protective services agency, and a communication line between the agency and the school to provide feedback and monitoring to protect the child.[11]

Once a report is filed it is also possible that the counselor will be called to testify in a later court proceeding. Counselors would be well-advised to consult with school legal counsel or another local attorney prior to such appearances to be adequately prepared.

CONTRIBUTING TO THE DELINQUENCY OF A MINOR

This topic is of primary concern to school counselors and those who work in practice with families and children. Other counselors also should be aware of the potential for contributing to the delinquency of a minor, however, and that a variety of acts can subject one to criminal liability for the offense. The majority of prosecutions for contributing to delinquency deal with people who patently attempt to subvert the morals of a juvenile. Even where such acts are unintentional, however, a counselor may not always be protected.

Contributing to the delinquency of a minor is not a common law offense. All states have enacted legislation of some form to protect children from any variation of the Fagin-Oliver Twist relationship.[12] Unfortunately, most state legislatures have not defined the specific conduct that constitutes the crime, and many jurisdictions leave it to the jury to determine whether a defendant's conduct was criminal.[13] A broad definition of the offense might include any actions that tend to injure the health, morals, or welfare of juveniles, or that encourage juveniles to participate in such actions. There is no certainty as to what constitutes this immoral conduct from state to state, however.

State courts are also divided on the question of intent. The traditional view is that a guilty intent, or *mens rea*, is a necessary element of the offense, but some states do not require *mens rea*. It is in these latter states that the danger of a counselor's inadvertently crossing the boundary of acceptable conduct is greatest. It is assumed that counselors would never deliberately do or encourage any act that would harm a minor. It is the inadvertent act, committed in the mistaken belief that it is legal, and, more important, that it is in the best interest of the client, that causes concern. It is not possible in this book to analyze the laws of each state, so to avoid such liability counselors must research the law in the state(s) in which they practice, and keep abreast of any changes in the statutes or cases that may occur.

SEXUAL MISCONDUCT

As described in chapter 4, a sexual relationship between a counselor and a client is clearly unethical, and may form the basis of an action for professional malpractice or negligence. In many states such conduct also constitutes a criminal offense, although a separate criminal suit must be prosecuted. The laws vary among the states in the requirements of this offense as well. In Minnesota, for example, sexual conduct with a patient is prohibited regardless of the client's consent.[14] Some states also prosecute such relations as rape, or statutory rape in the case of a minor client. In each case specific penalties are prescribed as punishment, and in some states victim compensation may also be required.

It should be obvious that sexual relationships between professional counselors and clients are never appropriate. It should also be obvious from this chapter that counselors who conduct themselves in a professional manner, and attempt to abide by the guidelines set out in the AACD *Ethical Standards*, are unlikely to incur criminal liability in their practice. It is imperative that counselors take every opportunity to inform themselves of the laws in the state(s) where they practice, and keep informed of changes as they occur.

References and Notes

1. State v. Woods, 307 N.C. 213, 297 S.E.2d 574 (1982).
2. Am.Jur.2d, *Criminal Law*, §172.
3. Counselors should be alert to changes in state criminal statutes that may affect potential liability. For example, a bill introduced in the Virginia General Assembly in 1984 would have required "educators," and presumably counselors, to report illegal drug use to law enforcement authorities. The bill was derailed on the house of delegates floor by delegates who feared it would expose educators to civil suits.
4. 21 Am.Jur.2d, *Criminal Law*, §174.
5. In State v. Potter, 19 S.E.2d 257 (N.C. 1942), the defendant merely misinformed police as to what had transpired at the scene of a stabbing and provided a ride for the felon. The court interpreted these as acts that gave aid and advantage to a criminal, thus sustaining the charge as accessory after the fact.
6. McClain v. State, 268 A.2d 572 (Md. 1970).
7. United States v. Foy, 416 F.2d 940 (7th Cir. 1969).
8. State v. Hoester, 681 S.W.2d 449 (Mo. 1984).
9. Howell-Nigrelli, J. (1988). Shared responsibility for reporting child abuse cases: A reaction to Spiegel. *Elementary School Guidance & Counseling, 22,* 289–290.
10. Watson, M.A., & Levine, J.D., (1989). Psychotherapy and mandated reporting of child abuse. *American Journal of Orthopsychiatry, 59*(2), 246.
11. Sandberg, D.N., Crabbs, S.K., & Crabbs, M.A., (1988). Legal issues in child abuse: Questions and answers for counselors. *Elementary School Guidance & Counseling, 22,* 268. [This article explains the policy considerations and legal issues in this area in greater detail.]
12. State v. Crary, 155 N.E.2d 262 (Ohio 1959).
13. See Contributing to delinquency, *Mens Rea,* 31 A.L.R.3d 848–867, for an in-depth study of the offense. See also 47 Am.Jur.2d, *Juvenile Courts*, §63–69.
14. Minnesota Criminal Sexual Conduct Code, Minn. Stat. Ann. §609.341–3471 (1985), as cited in Hotelling, K. (1988). Ethical, legal, and administrative options to address sexual relationships between counselor and client. *Journal of Counseling and Development, 67,* 233–237.

Chapter 6

THE PRIVATE PRACTITIONER

Counselors, like everyone else, must make the important decision, at one or more points in life, whether to practice as an employee or in a private capacity. This decision will be guided by a variety of factors, not the least of which are the personality of the individual (including the extent to which he or she is willing to take risks), marital and family status, financial circumstances, and security needs. For some, the steady income and other security resulting from being employed by another is of paramount importance, whereas for others, the freedom of being "one's own boss" is the overriding factor.

At the same time, counselors who desire to pursue their careers as private practitioners face an array of choices posed by federal and state law and manifested in a jumble of governmental requirements and forms that are spared those who elect to let their employer cope with those responsibilities. The purpose of this chapter is to provide some guidance through the regulatory labyrinth for those who are contemplating or have chosen the route of private practice.

OPERATIONAL FORM

As mundane as it may seem, one of the most fundamental choices the private practitioner faces is the option of operational form. A threshold decision is whether to function for profit or as a nonprofit entity. Many services provided by the counseling profession can be (and are) housed in nonprofit organizations, and this approach can offer a host of advantages, not the least of which is tax-exempt status. However, a separate portion of this chapter is devoted to the nonprofit approach; thus the assumption is made at this point that the practitioner will function as a business, in a for-profit capacity.

Although many practices are incorporated, this is by no means mandatory. Another option is the unincorporated, sole proprietorship. Of course, where two or more counselors are in the same practice, the alternative to incorporating is forming a partnership. Again, whether one practices alone or as part of a group is a matter that involves personality and economic circumstances, rather than simply considerations of law. But whether one chooses to operate a counseling practice in one business form rather than another is very much dictated by legal considerations.

55

A chief determinant in this regard is personal liability—or, more accurately, the avoidance of it. As a general proposition, the corporate form provides a shield against personal liability. This is the case regardless of whether the individual involved is a director, officer, or employee of the corporation. Under the law, the corporation is a separate legal entity that bears its own liability. Hence, the assets of the individual or individuals involved are generally immune from the reach of creditors and others who may initiate lawsuits.

The principal factors determining the business form are likely to be the perceived exposure to personal liability, the tax aspects (discussion follows), and the stringencies of creating and maintaining incorporation under the appropriate state's law. In some instances, some or all of any potential legal liability can be addressed by insurance. If the choice is the corporate form, the incorporators must adhere strictly to the law of the state of incorporation, usually the state in which the counseling function is principally to take place. If counseling is to be undertaken in one or more additional states, the corporation will probably have to qualify in the other jurisdictions in order to do business as a "foreign corporation."

It is important to stress that incorporation is not mandatory. There are some disadvantages to incorporation, but rarely are the initial costs or annual filing fees one of them. Instead, the disadvantages generally lie with the formalities necessary to maintain the corporate form. These include separating the financial records of the shareholders and the corporation, holding regular meetings of shareholders and directors, issuing stock and maintaining stock transfer records, and filing annual reports. As to the advantages offered by limited liability, this feature remains intact only as long as the corporate formalities are preserved. Failure to adhere to these formalities can mean loss of corporate status and thus loss of the protection against personal liability.

The corporate form is usually advantageous where there are risks of tort liabilities and where insurance is inadequate, unavailable, or expensive—an advantage that is rarely useful for counselors (see chapter 4). Also, a corporation can itself go through bankruptcy, meaning that personal bankruptcy need not occur should the practice fail. Although a corporation can be an independent borrower, however, most lending institutions will not make loans to a closely held corporation in the absence of one or more personal guarantees.

In some states, if the corporate form is selected, the counseling practice may be set up as a "professional corporation," rather than organized as a standard business corporation.

The differentiation made thus far between the private practitioner and the employee should not obscure a fundamental point: An individual or a group of individuals may own the counseling "business" and simultaneously be an employee or employees of that business.

GOVERNING INSTRUMENTS

Regardless of which operational form is chosen, a business entity must be governed by two operating instruments: the document by which it is created and the one stating its operational rules. For a corporation, the document by which it is created is its "articles of incorporation," the contents of which are dictated principally by state law. A corporation's operating rules are contained in its "bylaws." For a partnership, the creating document is the "partnership agreement," and a set of bylaws or other rules may be promulgated to guide its operations.

OWNERSHIP AND GOVERNANCE

Every business has its owner or owners. One who has an ownership interest in a business has an "equity" interest in the enterprise. Ownership of a corporation is evidenced by stock. These shares of ownership are represented by certificates. Without a stockholders' agreement or other restriction, shares of stock in a corporation may be freely transferred. These shares may also increase in value. In some cases, the feature of transferability of ownership, coupled with the potential for increases in equity, is perceived as an advantage of the corporate form. Partnership interests are equity holdings also. Unlike stock, however, partnership interests are usually encumbered by restrictions in the partnership agreement as to transferability.

Both the corporate form and the partnership form can produce either equality of ownership or "majority" (control) and "minority" interests. In either situation, a holding of an interest in a corporation or in a partnership is an asset (perhaps with an accompanying liability) to be reflected on the holder's personal financial statement. Every business entity must be governed by one or more individuals. The corporate form will be governed by a board of directors, with the board's functions delegated to an executive committee, officers, and staff. In a partnership, each of the partners may have a governing role, or governance may be vested in an elected committee.

ORGANIZATIONAL ASPECTS

In forming a business entity, a number of organizational formalities must be followed. Among these are an organizational meeting, with its proceedings recorded in minutes. At this meeting, an organizational structure will be selected, bank accounts authorized, and a lawyer and accountant retained. The corporate form requires initial meetings of both the shareholders and the board of directors. At the initial meeting of a corporation, directors other than those named in the articles of incorporation may be elected, as well as the corporation's officers.

TAX CONSIDERATIONS

The choice of operational form has immense federal and state tax consequences. Although the activities of an unincorporated sole proprietorship are considered to be among the activities of the individual who administers the business, the corporation and the partnership are both regarded as separate legal entities. A corporation is also generally regarded as a separate taxable entity. By contrast, the partnership is not a taxable entity but is a "pass-through" vehicle whereby the partnership's income, tax deductions, tax credits, and losses are transferred to the partners in their personal capacities.

Consequently, one of the disadvantages of incorporation can be "double taxation," meaning that the corporation's net profits are taxed at the corporate level and then distributions to the shareholders, in the form of dividends, are taxed to the recipients. (Dividends paid by a corporation are not deductible items for the corporation.) Double taxation can be avoided by causing distributions to the owners of the enterprise to be treated as compensation (salary or bonuses), which are deductible items for the corporation, or by electing "subchapter S" corporation status for the practice. One advantage of incorporation, from a tax standpoint, is the ability of a corporation to accumulate profits for future use, taking advantage of tax rates that are usually lower than those imposed on individuals. Another advantage of incorporation is the ability to create and enjoy the benefits of a variety of retirement, profit-sharing, and deferred compensation plans.

The transfer of assets to a corporation upon formation is not a taxable event (see Internal Revenue Code (IRC) section 351). Therefore, neither a shareholder nor the corporation will experience any gain or loss as a result of the exchange. Also, the assets in the corporation enter with the tax basis they had when owned by the shareholders, and the basis in the stock received by the shareholders is the same as it was in the assets transferred.

The tax aspects of a sole proprietorship are reflected on a special schedule of the individual's personal tax return (Form 1040, Schedule C). A corporation files its own income tax return (Form 1120). A partnership does not file a tax return (because, as noted, it is not taxable) but instead files an information return (Form 1065), with each partner's allocable share of income, deductions, and credits reflected on Schedule K–1. The information from this schedule is transferred to each partner's individual tax return.

For a counseling practice that is likely to generate some tax losses in the early years (due not only to expenses in excess of income but also to extensive tax deductions for depreciation and investment tax credits resulting from initial acquisitions of furniture, equipment, and supplies), the foregoing may seem to present a rather stark choice: Either incorporate for liability purposes but lose the ability to write off tax losses personally, or enjoy the pass-through of the tax benefits but risk exposure of personal assets to a lawsuit. In fact, however, there is a way to have the advantages of both.

Although the option is not always appropriate or even available, a counseling practice can be organized as a small business or a subchapter S corporation (IRC sections 1371–1379). This is a federal tax law concept, which allows an enterprise to be created as a corporation under state law—thereby preserving the shield against personal liability—yet be treated as a partnership for federal tax law purposes. This means that the tax deductions and tax credits experienced by the corporation are not frozen at the corporate level but are passed along to the stockholders in their personal capacities.

To be an S corporation, a corporation must have these attributes: It must have no more than 35 shareholders; have no more than one class of stock, be owned exclusively by individuals (or estates or certain trusts), and have no shareholders who are nonresident aliens. All shareholders must consent to an election to make a corporation an S entity. The election is made at the time of organization for the subsequent tax year or on or before the fifteenth day of the third month of the taxable year. Although this form can have marvelous tax consequences as long as the tax losses are flowing, it is a classic two-edged sword in that all income flows through to the stockholders for tax purposes, even if they do not actually take the money.

One other tax law feature for the small enterprise pertains to how the disposition of the stock is taxed. For example, where the requisite written plan has been adopted, the seller of the stock at a gain would pay tax at the capital gain rates. However, as a result of the Tax Reform Act of 1986, which repealed the capital gains deduction, capital gain is taxed at the same rates as ordinary income. It should be noted that, as this is written, Congress is considering legislation that would restore a beneficial tax treatment of capital gains in relation to ordinary gains. If, on the other hand, the sale is at a loss, it can be characterized as an "ordinary" loss (IRC section 1244). To be eligible for this treatment, a corporation must have less than $1 million in capital after the sale of the stock.

Tax Deductions

Whenever a counselor's private practice is conducted as a separate business enterprise, such as a corporation or partnership, most if not all of the expenses incurred in the practice are deductible as business expenses (IRC section 162). Purchases of capital items will probably give rise to depreciation deductions (IRC section 162) and investment tax credits (IRC sections 167, 168, 38).

If the business is a standard corporation, the tax deductions and tax credits are claimed by the corporation itself. If the business form is a partnership or an S corporation, these tax benefits flow through to the partners or shareholders. When the counseling practice is conducted as a sole proprietorship, the counselor experiences the tax benefits personally.

Even though the counselor may be an employee of a large institution or of his or her closely held corporation, the counselor may incur nonreimbursed expenses in connection with the employment duties. Some of these expenses are tax deductible, whereas others, as noted, may have to be capitalized with the cost recovered through the depreciation allowance. Other expenses may be permanently nondeductible, such as personal, living, or family expenses (IRC section 262).

A variety of deductions are available to employees or business owners in their individual capacities irrespective of their status in relation to the business; consequently they are not discussed here. These items include deductions for medical expenses, charitable contributions (which can also be made by the business enterprise, however), casualty losses, interest expenses, and taxes.

In general, an individual can deduct all "ordinary and necessary" expenses paid or incurred in the conduct of a trade or business (IRC section 162). Employee business deductions may now be claimed as itemized deductions only. Employee business expenses must be reported on Form 2106 and itemized on Schedule A of Form 1040 in order to claim any deduction. In addition, these expenses are subject to a 2% of adjusted gross income floor, that is, in order to claim miscellaneous itemized deductions, such deductions must exceed 2% of the taxpayer's adjusted gross income. Business expenses that may be deducted include the cost of travel, meals, and lodging while away from home (IRC section 162(a)(2)), and certain expenses for education, automobile, organizational dues, office at home, entertainment, and depreciable items. Business-related meal and entertainment expenses are subject to an additional limitation on their deductibility. In general, only 80% of a taxpayer's meals and entertainment expenses are deductible.

Educational Expenses

An employee may deduct all expenses for education when undertaken for the purpose of (a) maintaining or improving a skill required in his or her employment or (b) meeting the express requirements of the employer or the requirements of law imposed as a condition to the employee's retention of an established employment relationship, status, or rate of compensation (Income Tax Regulation (Reg.) 1.162–5). Other educational expenses are considered personal and do not qualify as a business deduction. Nondeductible educational expenses are those that are (a) required of an individual in order to meet the minimum educational requirements for qualification in his or her employment or (b) for education that is part of a program of study an individual pursues that will lead to qualification for a new employment relationship.

An employee can deduct expenses incurred for refresher courses or for courses concerning current developments, such as specialized institutes or seminars, as well as for academic courses, as long as the program of study does not lead to the acquisition of an entirely new skill. If an employer reimburses tuition fees for an employee enrolled in an educational course that will be beneficial to a career in the employer's business, the reimbursement is income to the employee. Because these amounts also constitute deductible business expenses, however, they need not be reported on the employee's tax return. (If the employer pays the tuition fees directly to the educational organization, the amounts are noncompensatory to the employee—and nondeductible by the employee.)

If an employee travels away from home primarily to obtain education, the expenses of which are deductible as business expenses, expenditures for travel, meals, and lodging are also deductible. However, the portion of expenses attributable to incidental personal activities (such as sight-seeing) is not deductible. Also, if the employee's reasons for travel away from home are partly personal, only the employee's expenditures for travel, meals, and lodging that relate directly to the time actually spent in educational pursuits are deductible.

Travel Expenses

An employee may deduct expenses incurred in traveling, including reasonable amounts expended for meals, lodging, and incidental items such as telephone charges, while away from home overnight in the conduct of business (IRC section 162(a)(2)). The general standard for deducting travel expenses is that they must be reasonable and necessary in the conduct of, and be directly attributable to, the employee's business (Reg. section 1.162–2(a)). If a trip is undertaken for purposes other than business, travel fares and incidental expenses are considered personal expenses, and expenses for meals and lodging are deemed living expenses, neither of which are deductible. Nonetheless, expenses incurred while at a destination that are properly allocable to an employee's business are deductible even if the travel and expenses to and from the destination are nondeductible. Travel expenses paid or incurred by an employee in connection with a trip to a professional convention, seminar, or similar meeting may be deductible. The business purpose must be the primary purpose of the expense in order for the deduction to be available.

If a spouse accompanies an employee on a business trip, the expenses attributable to the spouse's travel are not deductible unless it can be adequately shown that his or her presence on the trip has a bona fide business purpose. Performance by the spouse of some incidental service, such as the occasional typing of notes, will not qualify the expenses as deductible business expenses. It has been held that, if the presence of a spouse on a business trip contributes directly to the success of the business, such as through assisting the employee or establishing close personal and business relationships with clients, the expenses attributable to the spouse's travel are deductible. It has also been held that it is not enough if the alleged business function of the employee's spouse is to be socially gracious.

Deductions for travel expenses (including meals and lodging) are not allowable unless the employee substantiates, by keeping adequate records or by providing sufficient evidence to corroborate his or her own statement, the amount of the expense, the time and place of travel, and the business purpose of the expense (IRC section 274(d)(1)). Travel expenses must be substantiated by an account book, diary, statement of expense, or similar record; each element of an expenditure must be recorded at or near the time it is incurred, and each expenditure must be documented by receipts, paid bills, or similar evidence (Reg. section 1.274–5(c)(2)). Special rules govern the deductibility of expenses incurred while attending a convention, seminar, or similar meeting held in a foreign country (IRC, section 274(h)).

Automobile Expenses

An employee can deduct the cost of maintaining an automobile if it is used in connection with his or her business. The deduction is allowable only if the expenses are ordinary and necessary, and only with respect to the portion of the automobile expenses attributable to business, as opposed to personal, use. The automobile expense deduction can be ascertained by (a) determining the total amount of automobile expenses incurred during the year involved and (b) computing the deductible portion and multiplying that amount by a percentage based on mileage for the year that reflects business use. Under an optional simplified method of computing the deductible cost of operating an automobile, the expense deduction may be determined by using a standard mileage rate. Form 2106 is used for computing and reporting deductible automobile expenses under either approach.

Costs that qualify as deductible automobile expenses include outlays for gasoline, oil, lubrication, washing, repairs, tires, supplies, parking fees, tools, taxes, license fees, and insurance. Deductible costs do not include the cost of the automobile nor replacements that either prolong the useful life of, or increase the value of, the vehicle; the cost of those items must be recovered through allowances for depreciation. In computing deductible expenses with respect to an automobile used for business, an employee can include each year an amount representing a portion of the depreciation in value of the vehicle. This deduction is likewise confined to the portion of the cost of the automobile allocable to business use. Special rules limit the availability of the depreciation deduction in the case of luxury automobiles (IRC section 280F).

Office at Home Expenses

As noted, a deduction is usually not allowed for personal, living, or family expenses. For this reason, expenses attributable to a taxpayer's use of a personal residence (other than for interest, certain taxes, and casualty losses) are generally not deductible. If, however, a portion of an employee's personal residence is definitely and clearly set aside for office space and is used exclusively and regularly as an office, at least a portion of the expenses of the residence allocable to the office space should be deductible.

To take a deduction for using part of a home for a business, that part must be used exclusively and regularly: (1) as the principal place of business for any trade or business in which the taxpayer engages; (2) as a place to meet or deal with patients or clients in the normal course of the taxpayer's trade or business; (3) in connection with the taxpayer's trade or business, if using a separate structure that is not attached to the house or residence; and (4) in addition, if the taxpayer is an employee, rather than self-employed, the business use of the taxpayer's home must be for the convenience of the employer, based on a facts and circumstances test (IRC section 280(A)).

If, in the normal course of business, the taxpayer meets patients or clients in his or her home, even though the taxpayer may also carry on business at another location, the expenses for the part of the home used exclusively and regularly for this business activity are deductible. This applies only to office visits by clients, but does not apply to a room where the taxpayer receives phone calls. The part of the home that the taxpayer uses exclusively and regularly to meet patients or clients does not have to be the taxpayer's principal place of business. Counselors who maintain offices in their home generally meet this requirement.

This deduction involves a prorated portion of certain nondivisible expenses of the residence, such as property taxes, depreciation or rent, heat, electricity, other utilities, repairs, and insurance expenses. Starting in 1989, even if the taxpayer is in business, the cost of basic telephone service, including any taxes, may not be deducted for the first telephone line in the taxpayer's home. Long-distance charges directly related to the business use of the home, however, continue to be deductible. A full deduction may be obtained for repairs made directly to, or items purchased specifically for, the home office.

Even if home office expenses satisfy all the foregoing requirements, the allowable deduction for them cannot exceed the amount of gross income derived from the business use reduced by the allocable portion of the mortgage interest and real estate taxes deductions. These limitations do not defeat the deductions that remain available for home-related deductions, such as for mortgage interest, certain taxes, and casualty losses.

Entertainment Expenses

Expenses for entertainment are generally deductible, subject to the 80% limitation discussed above, if they qualify as ordinary and necessary business expenses. The deduction will not be allowed, however, unless the employee is also able to establish that the expenditure was directly related to the active conduct of business or, in the case of entertainment activity directly preceding or following a substantial and bona fide business discussion, the item was associated with the active conduct of business (IRC section 274 (a)(1)(A); Reg. section 1.274–2(a)(1)). In the case of a facility used in connection with entertainment, it must be shown that the facility was used primarily for the furtherance of the employee's business (IRC section 274(a)(1)(B)). Lavish or extravagant expenditures for entertainment are not allowed as a deduction (Reg. section 1.274–1).

The term "entertainment" means any activity that is generally considered to constitute amusement or recreation, such as entertaining business clients at night clubs, cocktail lounges, theaters, country clubs, golf and athletic clubs, sporting events, and on hunting, fishing, vacation, and similar trips. To satisfy the "directly related" test, it must be shown that (a) at the time the expenditure was made, the employee had more than a general expectation of deriving income or other specific business benefit at some indefinite time, (b) during the entertainment period to which the expenditure is related, the employee actively engaged in or reasonably expected to engage in a bona fide business transaction (e.g., a meeting or negotiations) for the purpose of obtaining a business benefit; (c) the principal character or aspect of the combined business and entertainment to which the expenditure was related was the active conduct of the employee's business; and (d) the expenditure was allocable to the employee and to a person or persons with whom he or she engaged in the active conduct of business during the entertainment, or with whom the employee would have engaged in such active conduct of business if it were not for circumstances beyond his or her control (Reg. section 1.274–2(c)(3)).

An expenditure for entertainment will also be considered directly related to the active conduct of an employee's business if it is established that the expenditure was for entertainment occurring in a clear business setting directly in furtherance of such business (Reg. section 1.274–2(c)(4)). In this instance an employee must clearly establish that any recipient of the entertainment would have reasonably known that the employee had no significant motive in incurring the expenditure other than directly furthering his or her business or that there was no meaningful personal or social relationship between the employee and the recipients of the entertainment.

An expenditure for entertainment will generally not be considered to be directly related to the active conduct of an employee's business if the entertainment occurred under circumstances in which there was little or no possibility of doing so. Such circumstances might include (a) events at which the employee was not present; (b) situations in which the distractions were substantial, such as a meeting or discussion at a nightclub, theater, or sporting event; and (c) social gatherings, or groups including people other than business associates, at places such as cocktail lounges, country clubs, golf and athletic clubs, or vacation resorts (Reg. section 1.274–2(c)(4)). An employee may, however, rebut these presumptions by clearly establishing that such expenditures were directly related to the active conduct of business. A strict reading of the law requires that, even where the entertainment deduction is otherwise established, an employee should refrain from deducting that portion of the expense that he or she normally would have spent in any case, such as the employee's portion of a luncheon or dinner bill. This rule seems to be enforced only in instances of abuse, however.

As noted, expenses of an entertainment activity that directly precedes or follows a substantial and bona fide business discussion are deductible if the item was associated with the active conduct of the employee's business (Reg. section 1.274–2(d)(1)). The entertainment is considered sufficiently associated with the active conduct of business if the employee establishes that he or she had a clear business purpose in making the expenditure, such as to obtain new business or to encourage the continuation of an existing business relationship (Reg. section 1.274–2(d)(2)). Whether any meeting, negotiation, or discussion constitutes a "substantial and bona fide business discussion" depends on the facts and circumstances of each case. It must be established that (a) the employee actively engaged in a business meeting, negotiation, discussion, or other bona fide business transaction, other than entertainment, for the purpose of obtaining income or other specific business benefit, and (b) the transaction was substantial in relation to the entertainment (Reg. section 1.274–2(d)(3)(i)). Entertainment that occurs on the same day as a substantial and bona fide business discussion is considered to directly precede or follow the discussion. Otherwise, the facts and circumstances of each case are considered, including the place, date, and duration of the business discussion;

whether the employee or the business associates are from out of town; the dates of arrival and departure of out-of-town associates; and the reasons why the entertainment did not take place on the day of the business discussion (Reg. section 1.274–2(d)(3)(ii)).

An expenditure for a facility used in connection with entertainment may also be deductible as a business expense. Personal or real property owned, rented, or used by an employee will be considered a "facility used in connection with entertainment" if it is used for or in connection with entertainment, unless such use is only incidental and insubstantial (Reg. section 1.274–2(e)(2)). Examples of such property include yachts, hunting lodges, fishing camps, swimming pools, tennis courts, bowling alleys, automobiles, airplanes, apartments, hotel suites, and homes in vacation resorts (Reg. section 1.274–2(e)(2)(i)). Examples of expenditures for entertainment facilities include depreciation; operating costs (e.g., rent and utility charges); expenses for the maintenance, preservation, or protection of a facility (e.g., repairs, painting, and insurance charges); salaries or expenses for subsistence paid to caretakers or guards; and losses realized on a sale or other disposition of a facility.

As noted, in order to be deductible, the expenses of a facility used in connection with entertainment must not only be directly related to the active conduct of the employee's business, but the facility also must be used primarily for the furtherance of such business (Reg. section 1.274–2(a)(2)). Again, all the facts and circumstances will be considered in applying the primary use test. Generally, it is the actual use of the facility that establishes the deductibility of expenditures with respect to it, rather than its availability for use or the employee's principal purpose in acquiring it. Primary use is generally deemed established if an employee can show use in furtherance of business in excess of 50% of total use (Reg. section 1.273.2(e)(4)).

Deductions based on entertainment expenses are not allowable unless the employee substantiates by adequate records or by sufficient evidence corroborating his or her own statement the amount of the expense, the time and place of the entertainment, amusement, recreation, or use of the facility, the business purpose of the expense, and the business relationship to the employee of the persons entertained or using the facility (IRC section 274(d)(2),(3)). Entertainment expenses must be substantiated by an account book, diary, statement of expense, or similar record; each expense must be recorded at or near the time it is incurred; and each item must be documented by receipts, paid bills, or similar evidence for an expenditure of $25 or more (Reg. section 274–5(c)(2)).

Substantiation Requirements

The Internal Revenue Service may require an employee to substantiate such information concerning deductions based on expenses as may seem to be pertinent in determining tax liability. Ordinarily, however, substantiation of expense account information is required only of the following categories of taxpayers: (a) those who are not required to account to their employer or who do not account, (b) those whose business expenses exceed the total amounts charged to or received from their employer and who claim a deduction for the excess, and (c) those whose employers are deemed to have inadequate accounting procedures for the reporting and substantiation of expenses by employees (Reg. section 1.162–17). One method of substantiating expenses incurred by an employee in connection with his or her employment is through the maintenance of a diary or record of expenditures, kept in sufficient detail to enable identification of the amount and nature of an expenditure. The employee should also preserve supporting documents, especially in connection with large or exceptional expenditures.

An employee who incurs expenses for business reasons may be wholly reimbursed, partially reimbursed, or not reimbursed at all by his or her employer. Certain requirements are imposed in connection with the federal income tax return of employees. An employee need not report on a tax return expenses incurred solely for the benefit of the employer for which the employer is required to account, which are charged directly or indirectly to the employer, or for which the employee is paid through advances, reimbursements, or otherwise, provided that the total of the amount of the payments is equal to the expenses incurred. However, in this case, the employee must state in the return that the total amounts charged to or received from the employer as advances or reimbursements did not exceed the employee's ordinary and necessary business expenses.

Should the total of amounts charged to or received from the employer be in excess of the ordinary and necessary business expenses incurred by the employee, and the employee accounts to the employer for the expenses, the employee must include the excess as part of his or her gross income. Again, the employee must so state in the tax return. However, to claim a business deduction for the excess, the employee must submit a statement (Form 2106) as part of the tax return showing the following: (a) the total of any charges borne by the employer and of any other amounts received from the employer for payment of expenses, whether by means of advances, reimbursements, or otherwise; (b) the nature of his or her occupation; (c) the number of days away from home on business; and (d) the total amount of ordinary and necessary business expenses incurred, broken down into broad categories such as transportation, meals, and lodging while away from home overnight, entertainment expenses, and other business expenses.

If an employee is not required to account to an employer for ordinary and necessary business expenses, or, if required, fails to account for the expenses, the employee must submit a statement as part of his or her return showing the same information as the employee who does not account to the employer. However, the difference in this situation is that the amounts of all advances or reimbursements must be reported by the employee as gross income, and expenses incurred should be shown as deductions on the return, with any excess of advances or reimbursements over expenses entered as income from "other" sources. Thus, an employee who is reimbursed in the amount of his or her outlays for business purposes, where the expenditures do not exceed reimbursements, and the employee accounts to the employer, is relieved of any obligation to report the expenses on the federal income tax return.

NONPROFIT ORGANIZATIONS

The foregoing discussion is predicated on the assumption that the counselor's private practice is conducted by means of a for-profit (business) entity. However, the work of the counselor may well be appropriate for another form: a nonprofit organization. For counselors, the choice of operational form in this context is the nonprofit corporation or unincorporated association. There is no such thing as a nonprofit partnership.

The unincorporated nonprofit is formed by adopting the creating document—a "constitution"—and thereafter some operational rules, namely, bylaws. If the nonprofit corporation is the vehicle, the governing instruments are the same as discussed above: articles of incorporation and bylaws. Nearly all states have a nonprofit corporation act (to be contrasted with a business corporation act) under which the nonprofit corporation may be formed. The decision to incorporate essentially involves the same considerations in the nonprofit setting as in the for-profit setting. Also, the governance aspects are the same in that the nonprofit entity will have a board of directors and officers.

A fundamental myth should be dispelled at this point: To be nonprofit does not mean that the enterprise cannot earn a "profit" in a financial or accounting sense. (Indeed, many nonprofit organizations are quite profitable in that regard.) The basic characteristic distinguishing a nonprofit from a for-profit is that the former cannot have underlying equity holders (such as shareholders) to whom net earnings are paid in the form of something akin to dividends.

The nonprofit form is the most appropriate if the counselor is motivated less by an objective of building a business and more by the prospect of operating a program with emphasis on research, publications, seminars, or the provision of certain types of counseling services. Again, this approach does not preclude a counselor from "owning" the entity in the sense of controlling its board of directors or receiving money from it in the form of a (reasonable) salary, if an employee, or other payment, if an independent contractor.

There are many advantages to the nonprofit form. In many instances, the chief advantage is that the nonprofit organization can be exempt from federal income taxation (IRC section 501(a)). For the most part, tax exemption is available to organizations whose program or programs are within the bounds of what are considered charitable, educational, or scientific activities (IRC section 501(c)(3)), although the entity may also qualify as a social welfare organization (IRC section 501(c)(4)). The meaning of the term "charitable" is manifold; it can embrace objectives such as the promotion of health, the relief of the distressed or the impoverished, or the advancement of education or science. What is "educational" usually is a function of training and instruction, either of individuals or of the general public. The term "scientific" tends to be synonymous with research. If an organization can qualify for tax-exempt status under federal tax law, there probably is a comparable classification for it under state law and, where applicable, under local law.

For those organizations that qualify as charitable, educational, or scientific entities, a useful feature is the ability to attract contributions that are tax-deductible by the donors. Tax deductibility for charitable gifts is not only available for federal income tax purposes (IRC section 170), but also for estate and gift tax purposes (IRC sections 2055, 2522). Charitable fundraising can be an effective way to capitalize an organization and to continue to support its financial needs. (However, some states have charitable solicitation acts that may require the organization to register and to report annually to the state.) Organizations that qualify for tax exemption often also are eligible for other advantages. For example, for some organizations, a meaningful asset is the ability to mail at the special second-class or third-class postal rates.

Some tax-exempt organizations must adhere to certain limitations that usually are not otherwise applicable, such as constraints on lobbying and political activities. Tax-exempts must file an annual return with the IRS, although it is an information return rather than a tax return (IRC section 6033). If a tax-exempt organization receives revenue from a business activity that is unrelated to its tax-exempt function, it may have to pay a tax on that business revenue (IRC section 511–514). A counselor does not necessarily have to select wholly between the for-profit or nonprofit form. A counseling practice can be housed in a for-profit entity, with a tax-exempt organization affiliated with it.

LICENSURE

One aspect of private practice of prime interest to today's counselor is the matter of state licensure. At the present, seven states have licensing laws (Alabama, Arkansas, Florida, Idaho, North Carolina, Texas, and Virginia). However, there is interest in the subject nationwide. From a regulatory stand-point, a state licensing law usually provides for the issuance of a license to a qualified professional counselor. (An individual may be able to practice without being a professional counselor, however, under the supervision of a professional counselor.) One of the prerequisites to qualification is that the individual must pass an examination, conducted under the auspices of a board of examiners. The license must be renewed periodically. The board of examiners is usually empowered to revoke or suspend a license, or to otherwise discipline a professional counselor in the event of certain circumstances. Due process requirements are embodied in the law.

These statutes also create the board of examiners, state the eligibility of those who may be appointed to the board, and delineate its functions. State licensing laws exempt from their purview the counseling activities for those who function as employees. Those who serve within certain stated professions, such as medicine, law, social work, and psychology, are also exempted from the requirements of these laws.

Counselor licensing laws have come into being only in recent years (Warner, Brooks, & Thompson, 1980) and reflect a tension in the regulatory setting between counseling and other professions, chiefly psychology and social work. Licensing laws also reflect the emergence of counseling as a private practice, rather than as solely the domain of employees of educational institutions and other agencies. These laws protect counselors against those who would enjoin their practice unless the counselors can also qualify as another type of practitioner, principally as psychologists. Indeed, the origin of these laws includes a court opinion holding that counselors cannot practice without a license in psychology (*Weldon v. Board of Psychologist Examiners*, 1982).

The first counselor licensing law was enacted in 1976 in the Commonwealth of Virginia. This statute was the product of intense work by the counseling profession, and six laws have subsequently been adopted (McFadden & Brooks, 1984). The licensing movement, which continues as a high priority of the profession, is part of the larger evolution of professional identity, role, function, and preparation.

PROFESSIONAL LIABILITY INSURANCE

It is hoped that the foregoing pages do not present too bleak a legal picture for counselors. Evidently, the opportunities for finding a counselor to be liable are on the increase, as are the numbers of people who are poised to sue in pursuit of damages. Although the ultimate answer is for counselors to conduct themselves in a manner that discourages even the potential for liability, the foregoing pages indicate that this is not always a simple objective. Insurance, however, is another affirmative defense available to counselors.

Counselors are generally aware of insurance in a variety of contexts, ranging from health and accident coverage to property, title, and life insurance protection. Professional liability insurance is another form of protection that is becoming more widely available and common in the counseling profession. The term *professional liability insurance* actually covers (or should cover) two distinct types of liability: (a) malpractice, the commission of an unprofessional act or failure to act in the course of a counselor's professional performance or as a result of counseling duties; and (b) injury to another, in the sense of a physical injury. Insurance policies are available that provide protection for counselors should professional liability, or the threat of it, arise. Counselors should pay particular attention to these features of any professional liability insurance policy:

1. The scope of coverage (the paragraph(s) titled "Exclusions" may be a large segment of the policy);
2. The monetary limits of coverage for liability;
3. The cost; and
4. Who selects legal counsel.

The American Association for Counseling and Development, through its Insurance Trust, sponsors a plan of professional and personal liability insurance for its members. For details of the program, write to the AACD Insurance Trust, 5999 Stevenson Avenue, Alexandria, VA 22304

References

McFadden, J., & Brooks, D., Jr. (1984). *Counselor licensure action packet*. Alexandria, VA: American Association for Counseling and Development.
Warner, Jr., Brooks, D. Jr., & Thompson (Eds.). (1980). *Counselor licensure: Issues and perspectives*. Alexandria, VA: American Personnel and Guidance Association.

Appendices

APPENDIX A

Ethical Standards of the American Association for Counseling and Development (1988)

PREAMBLE

The Association is an educational, scientific, and professional organization whose members are dedicated to the enhancement of the worth, dignity, potential, and uniqueness of each individual and thus to the service of society.

The Association recognizes that the role definitions and work settings of its members include a wide variety of academic disciplines, levels of academic preparation, and agency services. This diversity reflects the breadth of the Association's interest and influence. It also poses challenging complexities in efforts to set standards for the performance of members, desired requisite preparation or practice, and supporting social, legal, and ethical controls.

The specification of ethical standards enables the Association to clarify to present and future members and to those served by members the nature of ethical responsibilities held in common by its members.

The existence of such standards serves to stimulate greater concern by members for their own professional functioning and for the conduct of fellow professionals such as counselors, guidance and student personnel workers, and others in the helping professions. As the ethical code of the Association, this document establishes principles that define the ethical behavior of Association members. Additional ethical guidelines developed by the Association's Divisions for their specialty areas may further define a member's ethical behavior.

Section A: General

1. The member influences the development of the profession by continuous efforts to improve professional practices, teaching, services, and research. Professional growth is continuous throughout the member's career and is exemplified by the development of a philosophy that explains why and how a member functions in the helping relationship. Members must gather data on their effectiveness and be guided by the findings. Members recognize the need for continuing education to ensure competent service.

2. The member has a responsibility both to the individual who is served and to the institution within which the service is performed to maintain high standards of professional conduct. The member strives to maintain the highest levels of professional services offered to the individuals to be served. The member also strives to assist the agency, organization, or institution in providing the highest caliber of professional services. The acceptance of employment in an institution implies that the member is in agreement with the general policies and principles of the institution. Therefore the professional activities of the member are also in accord with the objectives of the institution. If, despite concerted efforts, the member cannot reach agreement with the employer as to acceptable standards of conduct that allow for changes in institutional policy conducive to the positive growth and development of clients, then terminating the affiliation should be seriously considered.

3. Ethical behavior among professional associates, both members and nonmembers, must be expected at all times. When information is possessed that raises doubt as to the ethical behavior of professional colleagues, whether Association members or not, the member must take action to attempt to rectify such a condition. Such action shall use the institution's channels first and then use procedures established by the Association.

4. The member neither claims nor implies professional qualifications exceeding those possessed and is responsible for correcting any misrepresentations of these qualifications by others.

15. In establishing fees for professional counseling services, members must consider the

financial status of clients and locality. In the event that the established fee structure is inappropriate for a client, assistance must be provided in finding comparable services of acceptable cost.

6. When members provide information to the public or to subordinates, peers, or supervisors, they have a responsibility to ensure that the content is general, unidentified client information that is accurate, unbiased, and consists of objective, factual data.

7. Members recognize their boundaries of competence and provide only those services and use only those techniques for which they are qualified by training or experience. Members should only accept those positions for which they are professionally qualified.

8. In the counseling relationship, the counselor is aware of the intimacy of the relationship and maintains respect for the client and avoids engaging in activities that seek to meet the counselor's personal needs at the expense of that client.

9. Members do not condone or engage in sexual harassment which is defined as deliberate or repeated comments, gestures, or physical contacts of a sexual nature.

10. The member avoids bringing personal issues into the counseling relationship, especially if the potential for harm is present. Through awareness of the negative impact of both racial and sexual stereotyping and discrimination, the counselor guards the individual rights and personal dignity of the client in the counseling relationship.

11. Products or services provided by the member by means of classroom instruction, public lectures, demonstrations, written articles, radio or television programs, or other types of media must meet the criteria cited in these standards.

Section B:
Counseling Relationship

This section refers to practices and procedures of individual and/or group counseling relationships.

The member must recognize the need for client freedom of choice. Under those circumstances where this is not possible, the member must apprise clients of restrictions that may limit their freedom of choice.

1. The member's primary obligation is to respect the integrity and promote the welfare of the client(s), whether the client(s) is (are) assisted individually or in a group relationship. In a group setting, the member is also responsible for taking reasonable precautions to protect individuals from physical and/or psychological trauma resulting from interaction within the group.

2. Members make provisions for maintaining confidentiality in the storage and disposal of records and follow an established record retention and disposition policy. The counseling relationship and information resulting therefrom must be kept confidential, consistent with the obligations of the member as a professional person. In a group counseling setting, the counselor must set a norm of confidentiality regarding all group participants' disclosures.

3. If an individual is already in a counseling relationship with another professional person, the member does not enter into a counseling relationship without first contacting and receiving the approval of that other professional. If the member discovers that the client is in another counseling relationship after the counseling relationship begins, the member must gain the consent of the other professional or terminate the relationship, unless the client elects to terminate the other relationship.

4. When the client's condition indicates that there is clear and imminent danger to the client or others, the member must take reasonable personal action or inform responsible authorities. Consultation with other professionals must be used where possible. The assumption of responsibility for the client's(s') behavior must be taken only after careful deliberation. The client must be involved in the resumption of responsibility as quickly as possible.

5. Records of the counseling relationship, including interview notes, test data, correspondence, tape recordings, electronic data storage, and other documents are to be considered professional information for use in counseling, and they should not be considered a part of the records of the institution or agency in which the counselor is employed unless specified by state statute or regulation. Revelation to others of counseling material must occur only upon the expressed consent of the client.

6. In view of the extensive data storage and processing capacities of the computer, the member must ensure that data maintained on a computer is: (a) limited to information that is appropriate and necessary for the services being provided; (b) destroyed after it is determined that the information is no longer of any value in providing services; and (c) restricted in terms of access to appropriate staff members involved in the provision of services by using the best computer security methods available.

7. Use of data derived from a counseling relationship for purposes of counselor training or research shall be confined to content that can be disguised to ensure full protection of the identity of the subject client.

8. The member must inform the client of the purposes, goals, techniques, rules of procedure, and limitations that may affect the relationship at or before the time that the counseling relationship is entered. When working with minors or persons who are unable to give consent, the member protects these clients' best interests.

9. In view of common misconceptions related to the perceived inherent validity of computer-generated data and narrative reports, the member must ensure that the client is provided with information as part of the counseling relationship that adequately explains the limitations of computer technology.

10. The member must screen prospective group participants, especially when the emphasis is on self-understanding and growth through self-disclosure. The member must maintain an awareness of the group participants' compatibility throughout the life of the group.

11. The member may choose to consult with any other professionally competent person about a client. In choosing a consultant, the member must avoid placing the consultant in a conflict of interest situation that would preclude the consultant's being a proper party to the member's efforts to help the client.

12. If the member determines an inability to be of professional assistance to the client, the member must either avoid initiating the counseling relationship or immediately terminate that relationship. In either event, the member must suggest appropriate alternatives. (The member must be knowledgeable about referral resources so that a satisfactory referral can be initiated.) In the event the client declines the suggested referral, the member is not obligated to continue the relationship.

13. When the member has other relationships, particularly of an administrative, supervisory, and/or evaluative nature with an individual seeking counseling services, the member must not serve as the counselor but should refer the individual to another professional. Only in instances where such an alternative is unavailable and where the individual's situation warrants counseling intervention should the member enter into and/or maintain a counseling relationship. Dual relationships with clients that might impair the member's objectivity and professional judgement (e.g., as with close friends or relatives) must be avoided and/or the counseling relationship terminated through referral to another competent professional.

14. The member will avoid any type of sexual intimacies with clients. Sexual relationships with clients are unethical.

15. All experimental methods of treatment must be clearly indicated to prospective recipients, and safety precautions are to be adhered to by the member.

16. When computer applications are used as a component of counseling services, the member must ensure that: (a) the client is intellectually, emotionally, and physically capable of using the computer application; (b) the computer application is appropriate for the needs of the client; (c) the client understands the purpose and operation of the computer application; and (d) a follow-up of client use of a computer application is provided to both correct possible problems (misconceptions or inappropriate use) and assess subsequent needs.

17. When the member is engaged in short-term group treatment/training programs (e.g., marathons and other encounter-type or growth groups), the member ensures that there is professional assistance available during and following the group experience.

18. Should the member be engaged in a work setting that calls for any variation from the above statements, the member is obligated to consult with other professionals whenever possible to consider justifiable alternatives.

19. The member must ensure that members of various ethnic, racial, religious, disability, and socioeconomic groups have equal access to computer applications used to support counseling services and that the content of available computer applications does not discriminate against the groups described above.

20. When computer applications are developed by the member for use by the general public as self-help/stand-alone computer software, the member must ensure that: (a) self-help computer applications are designed from the beginning to function in a stand-alone manner, as opposed to modifying software that was originally designed to require support from a counselor; (b) self-help computer applications will include within the program statements regarding intended user outcomes, suggestions for using the software, a description of the conditions under which self-help computer applications might not be appropriate, and a description of when and how counseling services might be beneficial; and (c) the manual for such applications will include the qualifications of the developer, the development process, validation data, and operating procedures.

Section C:
Measurement & Evaluation

The primary purpose of educational and psychological testing is to provide descriptive measures that are objective and interpretable in either comparative or absolute terms. The member must recognize the need to interpret the statements that follow as applying to the whole range of appraisal techniques including test and nontest data. Test results constitute only one of a variety of pertinent sources of information for personnel, guidance, and counseling decisions.

1. The member must provide specific orientation or information to the examinee(s) prior to and following the test administration so that the results of testing may be placed in proper perspective with other relevant factors. In so doing, the member must recognize the effects of socioeconomic, ethnic, and cultural factors on test scores. It is the member's professional responsibility to use additional unvalidated information carefully in modifying interpretation of the test results.

2. In selecting tests for use in a given situation or with a particular client, the member must consider carefully the specific validity, reliability, and appropriateness of the test(s). General validity, reliability, and related issues may be questioned legally as well as ethically when tests are used for vocational and educational selection, placement, or counseling.

3. When making any statements to the public about tests and testing, the member must give accurate information and avoid false claims or misconceptions. Special efforts are often required to avoid unwarranted connotations of such terms as IQ and grade equivalent scores.

4. Different tests demand different levels of competence for administration, scoring, and interpretation. Members must recognize the limits of their competence and perform only those functions for which they are prepared. In particular, members using computer-based test interpretations must be trained in the construct being measured and the specific instrument being used prior to using this type of computer application.

5. In situations where a computer is used for test administration and scoring, the member is responsible for ensuring that administration and scoring programs function properly to provide clients with accurate test results.

6. Tests must be administered under the same conditions that were established in their standardization. When tests are not administered under standard conditions or when unusual behavior or irregularities occur during the testing session, those conditions must be noted and the results designated as invalid or of questionable validity. Unsupervised or inadequately supervised test-taking, such as the use of tests through the mails, is considered unethical. On the other hand, the use of instruments that are so designed or standardized to be self-administered and self-scored, such as interest inventories, is to be encouraged.

7. The meaningfulness of test results used in personnel, guidance, and counseling functions generally depends on the examinee's unfamiliarity with the specific items on the test. Any prior coaching or dissemination of the test materials can invalidate test results. Therefore, test security is one of the professional obligations of the member. Conditions that produce most favorable test results must be made known to the examinee.

8. The purpose of testing and the explicit use of the results must be made known to the examinee prior to testing. The counselor must ensure that instrument limitations are not exceeded and that periodic review and/or retesting are made to prevent client stereotyping.

9. The examinee's welfare and explicit prior understanding must be the criteria for determining the recipients of the test results. The member must see that specific interpretation accompanies any release of individual or group test data. The interpretation of test data must be related to the examinee's particular concerns.

10. Members responsible for making decisions based on test results have an understanding of educational and psychological measurement, validation criteria, and test research.

11. The member must be cautious when interpreting the results of research instruments possessing insufficient technical data. The specific purposes for the use of such instruments must be stated explicitly to examinees.

12. The member must proceed with caution when attempting to evaluate and interpret the performance of minority group members or other persons who are not represented in the norm group on which the instrument was standardized.

13. When computer-based test interpretations are developed by the member to support the assessment process, the member must ensure that the validity of such interpretations is established prior to the commercial distribution of such a computer application.

14. The member recognizes that test results may become obsolete. The member will avoid and prevent the misuse of obsolete test results.

15. The member must guard against the appropriation, reproduction, or modification of published tests or parts thereof without acknowledgement and permission from the previous publisher.

16. Regarding the preparation, publication, and distribution of tests, reference should be made to:

a. "Standards for Educational and Psychological Testing," revised edition, 1985, published by the American Psychological Association on behalf of itself, the American Educational Research Association and the National Council of Measurement in Education.

b. "The Responsible Use of Tests: A Position Paper of AMEG, APGA, and NCME," *Measurement and Evaluation in Guidance*, 1972, 5, 385-388.

c. "Responsibilities of Users of Standardized Tests," APGA, *Guidepost*, October 5, 1978, pp. 5-8.

Section D:
Research and Publication

1. Guidelines on research with human subjects shall be adhered to, such as:

a. *Ethical Principles in the Conduct of Research with Human Participants*, Washington, D.C.: American Psychological Association, Inc., 1982.

b. Code of Federal Regulation, Title 45, Subtitle A, Part 46, as currently issued.

c. *Ethical Principles of Psychologists*, American Psychological Association, Principle #9: Research with Human Participants.

d. Family Educational Rights and Privacy Act (the Buckley Amendment).

e. Current federal regulations and various state rights privacy acts.

2. In planning any research activity dealing with human subjects, the member must be aware of and responsive to all pertinent ethical principles and ensure that the research problem, design, and execution are in full compliance with them.

3. Responsibility for ethical research practice lies with the principal researcher, while others involved in the research activities share ethical obligation and full responsibility for their own actions.

4. In research with human subjects, researchers are responsible for the subjects' welfare throughout the experiment, and they must take all reasonable precautions to avoid causing injurious psychological, physical, or social effects on their subjects.

5. All research subjects must be informed of the purpose of the study except when withholding information or providing misinformation to them is essential to the investigation. In such research the member must be responsible for corrective action as soon as possible following completion of the research.

6. Participation in research must be voluntary. Involuntary participation is appropriate only when it can be demonstrated that participation will have no harmful effects on subjects and is essential to the investigation.

7. When reporting research results, explicit mention must be made of all variables and conditions known to the investigator that might affect the outcome of the investigation or the interpretation of the data.

8. The member must be responsible for conducting and reporting investigations in a manner that minimizes the possibility that results will be misleading.

9. The member has an obligation to make available sufficient original research data to qualified others who may wish to replicate the study.

10. When supplying data, aiding in the research of another person, reporting research results, or making original data available, due care must be taken to disguise the identity of the subjects in the absence of specific authorization from such subjects to do otherwise.

11. When conducting and reporting research, the member must be familiar with and give recognition to previous work on the topic, as well as to observe all copyright laws and follow the principles of giving full credit to all to whom credit is due.

12. The member must give due credit through joint authorship, acknowledgement, footnote statements, or other appropriate means to those who have contributed significantly to the research and/or publication, in accordance with such contributions.

13. The member must communicate to other members the results of any research judged to be of professional or scientific value. Results reflecting unfavorably on institutions, programs, services, or vested interests must not be withheld for such reasons.

14. If members agree to cooperate with another individual in research and/or publication, they incur an obligation to cooperate as promised in terms of punctuality of performance and will full regard to the completeness and accuracy of the information required.

15. Ethical practice requires that authors not submit the same manuscript or one essentially similar in content for simultaneous publication consideration by two or more journals. In addition, manuscripts published in whole or in substantial part in another journal or published work should not be submitted for publication without acknowledgement and permission from the previous publication.

Section E:
Consulting

Consultation refers to a voluntary relationship between a professional helper and help-needing individual, group, or social unit in which the consultant is providing help to the client(s) in defining and solving a work-related problem or potential problem with a client or client system.

1. The member acting as consultant must have a high degree of self-awareness of his/her own values, knowledge, skills, limitations, and needs in entering a helping relationship that involves human and/or organizational change and that the focus of the relationship be on the issues to be resolved and not on the person(s) presenting the problem.

2. There must be understanding and agreement between member and client for the problem definition, change of goals, and prediction of consequences of interventions selected.

3. The member must be reasonably certain that she/he or the organization represented has the necessary competencies and resources for giving the kind of help that is needed now or may be needed later and that appropriate referral resources are available to the consultant.

4. The consulting relationship must be one in which client adaptability and growth toward self-direction are encouraged and cultivated. The member must maintain this role consistently and not become a decision maker for the client or create a future dependency on the consultant.

5. When announcing consultant availability for services, the member conscientiously adheres to the Association's Ethical Standards.

6. The member must refuse a private fee or other remuneration for consultation with persons who are entitled to these services through the member's employing institution or agency. The policies of a particular agency may make explicit provisions for private practice with agency clients by members of its staff. In such instances, the clients must be apprised of other options open to them should they seek private counseling services.

Section F:
Private Practice

1. The member should assist the profession by facilitating the availability of counseling services in private as well as public settings.

2. In advertising services as a private practitioner, the member must advertise the services in a manner that accurately informs the public of professional services, expertise, and techniques of counseling available. A member who assumes an executive leadership role in the organization shall not permit his/her name to be used in professional notices during periods when he/she is not actively engaged in the private practice of counseling.

3. The member may list the following: highest relevant degree, type and level of certification and/or license, address, telephone number, office hours, type and/or description of services, and other relevant information. Such information must not contain false, inaccurate, mislead-

ing, partial, out-of-context, or deceptive material or statements.

4. Members do not present their affiliation with any organization in such a way that would imply inaccurate sponsorship or certification by that organization.

5. Members may join in partnership/corporation with other members and/or other professionals provided that each member of the partnership or corporation makes clear the separate specialties by name in compliance with the regulations of the locality.

6. A member has an obligation to withdraw from a counseling relationship if it is believed that employment will result in violation of the Ethical Standards. If the mental or physical condition of the member renders it difficult to carry out an effective professional relationship or if the member is discharged by the client because the counseling relationship is no longer productive for the client, then the member is obligated to terminate the counseling relationship.

7. A member must adhere to the regulations for private practice of the locality where the services are offered.

8. It is unethical to use one's institutional affiliation to recruit clients for one's private practice.

Section G:
Personnel Administration

It is recognized that most members are employed in public or quasi-public institutions. The functioning of a member within an institution must contribute to the goals of the institution and vice versa if either is to accomplish their respective goals or objectives. It is therefore essential that the member and the institution function in ways to: (a) make the institutional goals specific; and public; (b) make the member's contribution to institutional goals specific; and (c) foster mutual accountability for goal achievement.

To accomplish these objectives, it is recognized that the member and the employer must share responsibilities in the formulation and implementation of personnel policies.

1. Members must define and describe the parameters and levels of their professional competency.

2. Members must establish interpersonal relations and working agreements with supervisors and subordinates regarding counseling or clinical relationships, confidentiality, distinction between public and private material, maintenance and dissemination of recorded information, work

load, and accountability. Working agreements in each instance must be specified and made known to those concerned.

3. Members must alert their employers to conditions that may be potentially disruptive or damaging.

4. Members must inform employers of conditions that may limit their effectiveness.

5. Members must submit regularly to professional review and evaluation.

6. Members must be responsible for in-service development of self and/or staff.

7. Members must inform their staff of goals and programs.

8. Members must provide personnel practices that guarantee and enhance the rights and welfare of each recipient of their service.

9. Members must select competent persons and assign responsibilities compatible with their skills and experiences.

10. The member, at the onset of a counseling relationship, will inform the client of the member's intended use of supervisors regarding the disclosure of information concerning this case. The member will clearly inform the client of the limits of confidentiality in the relationship.

11. Members, as either employers or employees, do not engage in or condone practices that are inhumane, illegal, or unjustifiable (such as considerations based on sex, handicap, age, race) in hiring, promotion, or training.

Section H:
Preparation Standards

Members who are responsible for training others must be guided by the preparation standards of the Association and relevant Division(s). The member who functions in the capacity of trainer assumes unique ethical responsibilities that frequently go beyond that of the member who does not function in a training capacity. These ethical responsibilities are outlined as follows:

1. Members must orient students to program expectations, basic skills development, and employment prospects prior to admission to the program.

2. Members in charge of learning experiences must establish programs that integrate academic study and supervised practice.

3. Members must establish a program directed toward developing students' skills, knowledge, and self-understanding, stated whenever possible in competency or performance terms.

4. Members must identify the levels of competencies of their students in compliance with relevant Division standards. These competencies must accommodate the paraprofessional as well as the professional.

5. Members, through continual student evaluation and appraisal, must be aware of the personal limitations of the learner that might impede future performance. The instructor must not only assist the learner in securing remedial assistance but also screen from the program those individuals who are unable to provide competent services.

6. Members must provide a program that includes training in research commensurate with levels of role functioning. Paraprofessional and technician-level personnel must be trained as consumers of research. In addition, personnel must learn how to evaluate their own and their program's effectiveness. Graduate training, especially at the doctoral level, would include preparation for original research by the member.

7. Members must make students aware of the ethical responsibilities and standards of the profession.

8. Preparatory programs must encourage students to value the ideals of service to individuals and to society. In this regard, direct financial remuneration or lack thereof must not be allowed to overshadow professional and humanitarian needs.

9. Members responsible for educational programs must be skilled as teachers and practitioners.

10. Members must present thoroughly varied theoretical positions so that students may make comparisons and have the opportunity to select a position.

11. Members must develop clear policies within their educational institutions regarding field placement and the roles of the student and the instructor in such placement.

12. Members must ensure that forms of learning focusing on self-understanding or growth are voluntary, or if required as part of the educational program, are made known to prospective students prior to entering the program. When the educational program offers a growth experience with an emphasis on self-disclosure or other relatively intimate or personal involvement, the member must have no administrative, supervisory, or evaluating authority regarding the participant.

13. The member will at all times provide students with clear and equally acceptable alternatives for self-understanding or growth experiences. The member will assure students that they have a right to accept these alternatives without prejudice or penalty.

14. Members must conduct an educational program in keeping with the current relevant guidelines of the Association.

APPENDIX B

Ethical Guidelines for Group Counselors (1989)

June 1, 1989 Final Draft
Approved by the Association for Specialists in Group Work (ASGW) Executive Board, June 1, 1989

Preamble

One characteristic of any professional group is the possession of a body of knowledge, skills, and voluntarily, self-professed standards for ethical practice. A Code of Ethics consists of those standards that have been formally and publicly acknowledged by the members of a profession to serve as the guidelines for professional conduct, discharge of duties, and the resolution of moral dilemmas. By this document, the Association for Specialists in Group Work (ASGW) has identified the standards of conduct appropriate for ethical behavior among its members.

The Association for Specialists in Group Work recognizes the basic commitment of its members to the Ethical Standards of its parent organization, the American Association for Counseling and Development (AACD) and nothing in this document shall be construed to supplant that code. These standards are intended to complement the AACD standards in the area of group work by clarifying the nature of ethical responsibility of the counselor in the group setting and by stimulating a greater concern for competent group leadership.

The group counselor is expected to be a professional agent and to take the processes of ethical responsibility seriously. ASGW views "ethical process" as being integral to group work and views group counselors as "ethical agents." Group counselors, by their very nature in being responsible and responsive to their group members, necessarily embrace a certain potential for ethical vulnerability. It is incumbent upon group counselors to give considerable attention to the intent and context of their actions because the attempts of counselors to influence human behavior through group work always have ethical implications.

The following ethical guidelines have been developed to encourage ethical behavior of group counselors. These guidelines are written for students and practitioners, and are meant to stimulate reflection, self-examination, and discussion of issues and practices. They address the group counselor's responsibility for providing information about group work to clients and the group counselor's responsibility for providing group counseling services to clients. A final section discusses the group counselor's responsibility for safeguarding ethical practice and procedures for reporting unethical behavior. Group counselors are expected to make known these standards to group members.

Ethical Guidelines

1. *Orientation and Providing Information:* Group counselors adequately prepare prospective or new group members by providing as much information about the existing or proposed group as necessary.

• Minimally, information related to each of the following areas should be provided.

(a) Entrance procedures, time parameters of the group experience, group participation expectations, methods of payment (where appropriate), and termination procedures are explained by the group counselor as appropriate to the level of maturity of group members and the nature and purpose(s) of the group.

(b) Group counselors have available for distribution, a professional disclosure statement that includes information on the group counselor's qualifications and group services that can be provided, particularly as related to the nature and purpose(s) of the specific group.

(c) Group counselors communicate the role expectations, rights, and responsibilities of group members and group counselor(s).

(d) The group goals are stated as concisely as possible by the group counselor including "whose" goal it is (the group counselor's, the institution's, the parent's, the law's, society's, etc.) and the role of group members in influencing or determining the group's goal(s).

(e) Group counselors explore with group members the risks of potential life changes that may occur because of the group experience and help members explore their readiness to face these possibilities.

(f) Group members are informed by the group counselor of unusual or experimental procedures that might be expected in their group experience.

(g) Group counselors explain, as realistically as possible, what services can and cannot be provided within the particular group structure offered.

(h) Group counselors emphasize the need to promote full psychological functioning and presence among group members. They inquire from prospective group members whether they are using any kind of drug or medication that may affect functioning in the group. They do not permit any use of alcohol and/or illegal drugs during group sessions and they discourage the use of alcohol and/or drugs (legal or illegal) prior to group meetings which may affect the physical or emotional presence of the member or other group members.

(i) Group counselors inquire from prospective group members whether they have ever been a client in counseling or psychotherapy. If a prospective group member is already in a counseling relationship with another professional person, the group counselor advises the prospective group member to notify the other professional of their participation in the group.

(j) Group counselors clearly inform group members about the policies pertaining to the group counselor's willingness to consult with them between group sessions.

(k) In establishing fees for group counseling services, group counselors consider the financial status and the locality of prospective group members. Group members are not charged fees for group sessions where the group counselor is not present and the policy of charging for sessions missed by a group member is clearly communicated. Fees for participating as a group member are contracted between group counselor and group member for a specified period of time.

Group counselors do not increase fees for group counseling services until the existing contracted fee structure has expired. In the event that the established fee structure is inappropriate for a prospective member, group counselors assist in finding comparable services of acceptable cost.

2. *Screening of Members:* The group counselor screens prospective group members (when appropriate to their theoretical orientation). Insofar as possible, the counselor selects group members whose needs and goals are compatible with the goals of the group, who will not impede the group process, and whose well-being will not be jeopardized by the group experience. An orientation to the group (i.e., ASGW Ethical Guideline #1), is included during the screening process.

• Screening may be accomplished in one or more ways, such as the following:

(a) Individual interview,

(b) Group interview of prospective group members,

(c) Interview as part of a team staffing, and

(d) Completion of a written questionnaire by prospective group members.

3. *Confidentiality:* Group counselors protect members by defining clearly what confidentiality means, why it is important, and the difficulties involved in enforcement.

(a) Group counselors take steps to protect members by defining confidentiality and the limits of confidentiality (i.e., when a group member's condition indicates that there is clear and imminent danger to the member, others, or physical property, the group counselor takes reasonable personal action and/or informs responsible authorities).

(b) Group counselors stress the importance of confidentiality and set a norm of confidentiality regarding all group participants' disclosures. The importance of maintaining confidentiality is emphasized before the group begins and at various times in the group. The fact that confidentiality cannot be guaranteed is clearly stated.

(c) Members are made aware of the difficulties involved in enforcing and ensuring confidentiality in a group setting. The counselor provides examples of how confidentiality can non-maliciously be broken to increase members' awareness, and helps to lessen the likelihood that this breach of confidence will occur. Group counselors inform group members about the potential consequences of intentionally breaching confidentiality.

(d) Group counselors can only ensure confidentiality on their part and not on the part of the members.

(e) Group counselors video or audio tape a group session only with the prior consent, and the members' knowledge of how the tape will be used.

(f) When working with minors, the group counselor specifies the limits of confidentiality.

(g) Participants in a mandatory group are made aware of any reporting procedures required of the group counselor.

(h) Group counselors store or dispose of group member records (written, audio, video, etc.) in ways that maintain confidentiality.

(i) Instructors of group counseling courses maintain the anonymity of group members whenever discussing group counseling cases.

4. *Voluntary/Involuntary Participation:* Group counselors inform members whether participation is voluntary or involuntary.

(a) Group counselors take steps to ensure informed consent procedures in both voluntary and involuntary groups.

(b) When working with minors in a group, counselors are expected to follow the procedures specified by the institution in which they are practicing.

(c) With involuntary groups, every attempt is made to enlist the cooperation of the members and their continuance in the group on a voluntary basis.

(d) Group counselors do not certify that group treatment has been received by members who merely attend sessions, but did not meet the defined group expectations. Group members are informed about the consequences for failing to participate in a group.

5. *Leaving a Group:* Provisions are made to assist a group member to terminate in an effective way.

(a) Procedures to be followed for a group member who chooses to exit a group prematurely are discussed by the counselor with all group members either before the group begins, during a pre-screening interview, or during the initial group session.

(b) In the case of legally mandated group counseling, group counselors inform members of the possible consequences for premature self termination.

(c) Ideally, both the group counselor and the member can work cooperatively to determine the degree to which a group experience is productive or counterproductive for that individual.

(d) Members ultimately have a right to discontinue membership in the group, at a designated time, if the predetermined trial period proves to be unsatisfactory.

(e) Members have the right to exit a group, but it is important that they be made aware of the importance of informing the counselor and the group members prior to deciding to leave. The counselor discusses the possible risks of leaving the group prematurely with a member who is considering this option.

(f) Before leaving a group, the group counselor encourages members (if appropriate) to discuss their reasons for wanting to discontinue membership in the group. Counselors intervene if other members use undue pressure to force a member to remain in the group.

6. *Coercion and Pressure:* Group counselors protect member rights against physical threats, intimidation, coercion, and undue peer pressure insofar as is reasonably possible.

(a) It is essential to differentiate between "therapeutic pressure" that is part of any group and "undue pressure," which is not therapeutic.

(b) The purpose of a group is to help participants find their own answer, not to pressure them into doing what the group thinks is appropriate.

(c) Counselors exert care not to coerce participants to change in directions which they clearly state they do not choose.

(d) Counselors have a responsibility to intervene when others use undue pressure or attempt to persuade members against their will.

(e) Counselors intervene when any member attempts to act out aggression in a physical way that might harm another member or themselves.

(f) Counselors intervene when a member is verbally abusive or inappropriately confrontive to another member.

7. *Imposing Counselor Values:* Group counselors develop an awareness of their own values and needs and the potential impact they have on the interventions likely to be made.

(a) Although group counselors take care to avoid imposing their values on members, it is appropriate that they expose their own beliefs, decisions, needs, and values, when concealing them would create problems for the members.

(b) There are values implicit in any group, and these are made clear to potential members before they join the group. (Examples of certain values include: expressing feelings, being direct and honest, sharing personal material with others, learning how to trust, improving interpersonal communication, and deciding for oneself.)

(c) Personal and professional needs of group counselors are not met at the members' expense.

(d) Group counselors avoid using the group for their own therapy.

(e) Group counselors are aware of their own values and assumptions and how these apply in a multicultural context.

(f) Group counselors take steps to increase their awareness of ways that their personal reactions to members might inhibit the group process and they monitor their countertransference. Through an awareness of the impact of sterotyping and discrimination (i.e., biases based on age, disability, ethnicity, gender, race, religion, or sexual preference), group counselors guard the individual rights and personal dignity of all group members.

8. *Equitable Treatment:* Group counselors make every reasonable effort to treat each member individually and equally.

(a) Group counselors recognize and respect differences (e.g., cultural, racial, religious, lifestyle, age, disability, gender) among group members.

(b) Group counselors maintain an awareness of their behavior toward individual group members and are alert to the potential detrimental effects of favoritism or partiality toward any particular group member to the exclusion or detriment of any other member(s). It is likely that group counselors will favor some members over others, yet all group members deserve to be treated equally.

(c) Group counselors ensure equitable use of group time for each member by inviting silent members to become involved, acknowledging nonverbal attempts to communicate, and discouraging rambling and monopolizing of time by members.

(d) If a large group is planned, counselors consider enlisting another qualified professional to serve as a co-leader for the group sessions.

9. *Dual Relationships:* Group counselors avoid dual relationships with group members that might impair their objectivity and professional judgment, as well as those which are likely to compromise a group member's ability to participate fully in the group.

(a) Group counselors do not misuse their professional role and power as group leader to advance personal or social contacts with members throughout the duration of the group.

(b) Group counselors do not use their professional relationship with group members to further their own interest either during the group or after the termination of the group.

(c) Sexual intimacies between group counselors and members are unethical.

(d) Group counselors do not barter (exchange) professional services with group members for services.

(e) Group counselors do not admit their own family members, relatives, employees, or personal friends as members to their groups.

(f) Group counselors discuss with group members the potential detrimental effects of group members engaging in intimate inter-member relationships outside of the group.

(g) Students who participate in a group as a partial course requirement for a group course are not evaluated for an academic grade based upon their degree of participation as a member in a group. Instructors of group counseling courses take steps to minimize the possible negative impact on students when they participate in a group course by separating course grades from participation in the group and by allowing students to decide what issues to explore and when to stop.

(h) It is inappropriate to solicit members from a class (or institutional affiliation) for one's private counseling or therapeutic groups.

10. *Use of Techniques:* Group counselors do not attempt any technique unless trained in its use or under supervision by a counselor familiar with the intervention.

(a) Group counselors are able to articulate a theoretical orientation that guides their practice, and they are able to provide a rationale for their interventions.

(b) Depending upon the type of an intervention, group counselors have training commensurate with the potential impact of a technique.

(c) Group counselors are aware of the necessity to modify their techniques to fit the unique needs of various cultural and ethnic groups.

(d) Group counselors assist members in translating in-group learnings to daily life.

11. *Goal Development:* Group counselors make every effort to assist members in developing their personal goals.

(a) Group counselors use their skills to assist members in making their goals specific so that others present in the group will understand the nature of the goals.
(b) Throughout the course of a group, group counselors assist members in assessing the degree to which personal goals are being met, and assist in revising any goals when it is appropriate.
(c) Group counselors help members clarify the degree to which the goals can be met within the context of a particular group.

12. *Consultation:* Group counselors develop and explain policies about between-session consultation to group members.

(a) Group counselors take care to make certain that members do not use between-session consultations to avoid dealing with issues pertaining to the group that would be dealt with best in the group.
(b) Group counselors urge members to bring the issues discussed during between-session consultations into the group if they pertain to the group.
(c) Group counselors seek out consultation and/or supervision regarding ethical concerns or when encountering difficulties which interfere with their effective functioning as group leaders.
(d) Group counselors seek appropriate professional assistance for their own personal problems or conflicts that are likely to impair their professional judgment and work performance.
(e) Group counselors discuss their group cases only for professional consultation and educational purposes.
(f) Group counselors inform members about policies regarding whether consultations will be held confidential.

13. *Termination from the Group:* Depending upon the purpose of participation in the group, counselors promote termination of members from the group in the most efficient period of time.

(a) Group counselors maintain a constant awareness of the progress made by each group member and periodically invite the group members to explore and reevaluate their experiences in the group. It is the responsibility of group counselors to help promote the independence of members from the group in a timely manner.

14. *Evaluation and Follow-up:* Group counselors make every attempt to engage in ongoing assessment and to design follow-up procedures for their groups.

(a) Group counselors recognize the importance of ongoing assessment of a group, and they assist members in evaluating their own progress.
(b) Group counselors conduct evaluation of the total group experience at the final meeting (or before termination), as well as ongoing evaluation.
(c) Group counselors monitor their own behavior and become aware of what they are modeling in the group.
(d) Follow-up procedures might take the form of personal contact, telephone contact, or written contact.
(e) Follow-up meetings might be with individuals, or groups, or both to determine the degree to which: (i) members have reached their goals, (ii) the group had a positive or negative effect on the participants, (iii) members could profit from some type of referral, and (iv) as information for possible modification of future groups. If there is no follow-up meeting, provisions are made available for individual follow-up meetings to any member who needs or requests such a contact.

15. *Referrals:* If the needs of a particular member cannot be met within the type of group being offered, the group counselor suggests other appropriate professional referrals.

(a) Group counselors are knowledgeable of local community resources for assisting group members regarding professional referrals.
(b) Group counselors help members seek further professional assistance, if needed.

16. *Professional Development:* Group counselors recognize that professional growth is a continuous, ongoing, developmental process throughout their career.

(a) Group counselors maintain and upgrade their knowledge and skill competencies through educational activities, clinical experiences, and participation in professional development activities.
(b) Group counselors keep abreast of research findings and new developments as applied to groups.

Safeguarding Ethical Practice and Procedures for Reporting Unethical Behavior

The preceding remarks have been advanced as guidelines which are generally representative of ethical and professional group practice. They have not been proposed as rigidly defined prescriptions. However, practitioners who are thought to be grossly unresponsive to the ethical concerns addressed in this document may be subject to a review of their practices by the AACD Ethics Committee and ASGW peers.

- For consultation and/or questions regarding these ASGW Ethical Guidelines or group ethical dilemmas, you may contact the Chairperson of the ASGW Ethics Committee. The name, address, and telephone number of the current ASGW Ethics Committee Chairperson may be acquired by telephoning the AACD office in Alexandria, Virginia at (703) 823-9800.
- If a group counselor's behavior is suspected as being unethical, the following procedures are to be followed:

  (a) Collect more information and investigate further to confirm the unethical practice as determined by the ASGW Ethical Guidelines.
  (b) Confront the individual with the apparent violation of ethical guidelines for the purposes of protecting the safety of any clients and to help the group counselor correct any inappropriate behaviors. If satisfactory resolution is not reached through this contact then:
  (c) A complaint should be made in writing, including the specific facts and dates of the alleged violation and all relevant supporting data. The complaint should be included in an envelope marked "CONFIDENTIAL" to ensure confidentiality for both the accuser(s) and the alleged violator(s) and forwarded to all of the following sources:

     1. The name and address of the Chairperson of the state Counselor Licensure Board for the respective state, if in existence.
     2. The Ethics Committee
        c/o The President

American Association for Counseling
and Development
5999 Stevenson Avenue
Alexandria, Virginia 22304

3. The name and address of all private credentialing agencies that the alleged violator maintains credentials or holds professional membership. Some of these include the following:

National Board for Certified
Counselors, Inc.
5999 Stevenson Avenue
Alexandria, Virginia 22304

National Council for Credentialing of
Career Counselors
c/o NBCC
5999 Stevenson Avenue
Alexandria, Virginia 22304

National Academy for Certified
Clinical Mental Health Counselors
5999 Stevenson Avenue
Alexandria, Virginia 22304

Commission on Rehabilitation
Counselor Certification
162 North State Street, Suite 317
Chicago, Illinois 60601

American Association for Marriage and
Family Therapy
1717 K Street, N.W., Suite 407
Washington, D.C. 20006

American Psychological Association
1200 Seventeenth Street, N.W.
Washington, D.C. 20036

American Group Psychotherapy
Association, Inc.
25 East 21st Street, 6th Floor
New York, New York 10010

APPENDIX C

AACD Legal Action Program (1987)

(Approved by AACD Governing Council, April 1987)

(The Legal Defense Program was established by the APGA Board of Directors, December 8–10, 1977 and revised by the Board of Directors, July 12–15, 1979. It was further revised by the AACD Governing Council April 1987)

I. Statement of Purpose

The AACD Legal Defense Program for AACD members was established by the APGA Board of Directors at its meeting, December 8–10, 1977, to assist members in their legal efforts to redress discrimination or unfair practices in employment related matters. In 1987, the AACD Governing Council revised the program and renamed it the Legal Action Program. The kind of legal disputes for which members (heretofore defined for the purposes of this program as AACD members in good standing with membership in at least one division, state or national divisions or state branches) may request financial assistance are cases in which facts are at issue that are deemed by the Review Panel to discriminate clearly against counselors in general or against the counseling profession. Cases will not be funded if a counselor's performance, judgement or competence is at issue, unless the Review Panel determines that the allegations, even if proven accurate, do not constitute unprofessional, unethical, or illegal conduct. For funding under this program to be authorized, an actual case must be pending. In civil suits, a bill of complaint and responsive pleadings must have been filed. In a criminal suit, charges must have been filed. In appellate cases, the appeal must have been filed.

The purpose of this program is to provide assistance to eligible AACD members to enable them to resolve legal disputes in matters relating to their primary responsibilities or interests in the area of counseling and human development [see AACD Bylaws, Article II, Section 2(a)].

An AACD member eligible for this program must be a member in good standing for at least one year prior to the onset of the legal dispute. State and national divisions and state branches are automatically eligible provided their charter has been current for one year.

II. Obtaining the Revenue for the Legal Action Program

A. The Governing Council establishes the budget and authorizes membership solicitation of additional voluntary contributions for the fund.

B. Policies and guidelines to govern the program's operation shall be the sole responsibility of the AACD Governing Council, based upon monitoring reports from the Counselor Advocacy Committee.

C. The Executive Director shall report the activities and the fiscal condition of the Program to the Governing Council at each meeting of the Council.

III. Review Panel and Guidelines

A. The President, Past President, Executive Director of AACD, President of the applicant's primary and most relevant division (subject to the desire of the applicant) and the Chair of the AACD Committee on Counselor Advocacy shall serve as a review panel for all applications for assistance from the Legal Action Program. AACD Counsel will serve as a consultant to the Review Panel. The Judgement of the Review Panel shall be made in accordance with the guidelines established by the AACD Governing Council.

1. Applicants seeking support from these funds will be notified of the decision of the Review Panel within sixty (60) working days of receipt of the application and all supporting documents.

2. Rejected applications may be appealed to the AACD Governing Council at its next meeting.

B. The guidelines for members obtaining financial support from this program include:

1. Two hundred and fifty dollars ($250) of legal fees and expenses must be paid by the AACD member.

2. After the $250 of legal expenses are paid by the member, a minimum of $250.00 shall be provided by any of the following:

a. state branch

b. state division

c. national division

d. professional or private source

3. After ascertaining that the expenditures made by the member and other sources total at least $500.00, a sum not to exceed $1,000.00 may be provided to the approved member from the AACD Legal Action Fund.

4. Should the receipted expenditures exceed the initial $1,000.00, costs above that $1,000.00 may be reimbursed up to an additional $4,000.00 sum per member per act or occurrence. If more than one member is involved in the same occurrence under litigation, only $5,000.00 payment will be authorized, except as determined by the AACD Governing Council.

5. Expenditures will be limited to the authorized sums in the legal action fund.

6. State or national divisions, and state branches may apply for up to $5,000.00 provided they have evidenced expenditure of or committed funds of a matching amount of money designated for such legal action.

7. If a funded case is appealed to a higher court, an additional $5,000.00 may be authorized.

C. Excluded from eligibility would be cases such as:

1. Non-professionally related criminal suits or charges.

2. Licensure outside of the counseling profession.

3. Professional liability suits.

4. Other cases determined by the Review Panel to be inappropriate for commitment of AACD Legal Action Funds.

IV. Application Procedures for Members

A. The AACD member requests from AACD Headquarters an "Application for Assistance from the AACD Legal Action Fund" claim. The completed claim forms are sent to the Executive Director. The member shall complete these forms during the legal proceedings. All forms, documentation and records shall be treated as confidential documents.

B. Upon receipt of the completed forms and supporting documents signed by the applicant, representing attorney, and official representative of the group contributing the additional $250.00 to guarantee expenditures of at least $500.00, the Executive Director will review all of the information in relation to the established policies and procedures and, then, submit this information to the Review Panel for determination of eligibility.

C. Once the eligibility for assistance is determined, the member will be notified and a check for the authorized amount, not to exceed the appropriate guidelines, will be authorized and mailed payable to the attorney.

D. If the Review Panel determines the member is ineligible for assistance, the member may appeal this decision to the AACD Governing Council. The Governing Council shall notify the member of the results of its deliberations, including the reasons for its actions.

E. Falsification of any document or the submission of any fraudulent statements or materials shall render the application null and void. If such falsification or fraudulence is discovered before or after payment is made, AACD reserves the right to take whatever action is necessary that is appropriate legally and ethically, to recover allocated funds or expenditures related to processing such an application.

AMERICAN ASSOCIATION FOR COUNSELING AND DEVELOPMENT

5999 Stevenson Avenue
Alexandria, VA 22304

APPLICATION FOR ASSISTANCE FROM THE AACD LEGAL ACTION FUND

Date of Application _____

AACD Membership Number _____

Name _____

Business Address _____

_____

Home Address _____

Business Phone _____ Home Phone _____

Brief Statement of Dispute:

In order for this application to be completed and reviewed, a copy of all pleadings filed in the case must be attached.

Which is your primary Division? _____

Do you wish to have Division President on Review Panel? ____ Yes ____ No

I hereby certify that I have contributed a minimum of $250.00 of my own personal funds to this case. I also hereby certify that all of the information in this application is true and correct to the best of my knowledge.

_____ _____

Date   Signature of Applicant

I hereby certify that I or my organization have contributed a minimum of $250.00 to the above-stated legal action. My signature indicates I have not provided any false or misleading information.

_____ _____

Signature   Organization

AMERICAN ASSOCIATION FOR COUNSELING AND DEVELOPMENT

5999 Stevenson Avenue
Alexandria, VA 22304

FINANCIAL AFFIDAVIT FOR AACD LEGAL ACTION FUND

Name of AACD Member _____

Name of Attorney _____

Attorney's Address _____

_____

Member's Address _____

_____

Statement of Legal Costs:

Received by Attorney $_____

Remaining Fees $_____

This information we hereby present is true and correct.

_____   Date _____
AACD Member's Signature

_____   Date _____
Member's Attorney's Signature

90

AMERICAN ASSOCIATION FOR COUNSELING AND DEVELOPMENT

5999 Stevenson Avenue
Alexandria, VA 22304

APPLICATION FOR ADDITIONAL ASSISTANCE FROM AACD LEGAL ACTION FUND

Date of Application _____

AACD Membership Number _____

Name _____

Business Address _____

_____

Home Address _____

Business Phone _____ Home Phone _____

Applications for additional assistance from AACD Legal Action Fund will not be considered unless one of the following conditions has been met:

1. An initial request for funds has been approved up to $1,000.00.
2. All possible assistance has been granted and the case is now in appeal.

Member Expenditure on Case to Date $_____

Sum of All Legal Action Funds Awarded to Date $_____

Statement of Total Sum of Attorney's Fees $_____

Status of Case? _____ initial proceedings _____ appellate proceedings

Amount(s) Granted from Other Sources $_____

The information we hereby present is true and correct.

_____ Date _____
AACD Member's Signature

_____ Date _____
Member's Attorney's Signature

The AACD Ethics Committee maintains and periodically updates an extensive Ethics Bibliography. To obtain a copy, write to:

ETHICS BIBLIOGRAPHY

American Association for Counseling and Development
5999 Stevenson Avenue
Alexandria, VA 22304

APPENDIX D

The Supreme Court and Abortion

Excerpts from the Supreme Court's opinion in *Akron v. Akron Center for Reproductive Health, Inc.* 462 U.S. 416, 103 S. Ct. 2481, 76 L.Ed.2d 687 (1983).

[14]"In *Roe v. Wade*, the Court held that the 'right of privacy . . . founded in the Fourteenth Amendment's concept of personal liberty and restrictions upon state action . . . is broad enough to encompass a woman's decision whether or not to terminate her pregnancy.' 410 U.S., at 153, 35 L.Ed.2d 147, S.Ct.705. Central among these protected liberties is an individual's 'freedom of personal choice in matters of marriage and family life' *Roe*, 410 U.S., at 169, 35 L.Ed.2d 147,93, S.Ct.705. . . The decision in *Roe* was based firmly on this long-recognized and essential element of personal liberty.

The Court also has recognized, because abortion is a medical procedure, that the full vindication of the woman's fundamental right necessarily requires that her physician be given 'the room he needs to make his best medical judgment.' Doe v. Bolton, 410 U.S.179, 192, 35 L.Ed.2d.201, 93 S.Ct. 739 (1973). . . . The physician's exercise of this medical judgment encompasses both assisting the woman in the decision making process and implementing her decision should she choose abortion . . . At the same time, the Court in *Roe* acknowledged that the woman's fundamental right 'is not unqualified and must be considered against important state interests in abortion.' . . . But restrictive state regulation of the right to choose abortion, as with other fundamental rights subject to searching judicial examination, must be supported by a compelling state interest . . . We have recognized two such interests that may justify state regulation of abortions. First, a State has an 'important and legitimate interest in protecting the potentiality of human life.' . . . Although the interest exists 'throughout the course of the woman's pregnancy,' it becomes compelling only at viability, the point at which the fetus 'has the capability of meaningful life outside the mother's womb.' . . . At viability this interest in protecting the potential life of the unborn child is so important that the State may proscribe abortions altogether, 'except when it is necessary to preserve the life or health of the mother.' . . . Second, because a State has a legitimate concern with the health of women who undergo abortions, 'a State may properly assert important interests in safeguarding health [and] in maintaining medical standards.' . . . We held in *Roe*, however, that this health interest does not become compelling until 'approximately the end of the first trimester' of pregnancy . . . Until that time, a pregnant woman must be permitted, in consultation with her physician, to decide to have an abortion and to effectuate that decision 'free of interference by the State' . . . From approximately the end of the first trimester of pregnancy, the State 'may regulate the abortion procedure to the extent that the regulation reasonably relates to the preservation and protection of maternal health.' . . . The State's discretion to regulate on this basis does not, however, permit it to adopt abortion regulations that depart from accepted medical practice . . . If a State requires licensing or undertakes to regulate the performance of abortions during this period, the health standards adopted must be 'legitimately related to the objective the States seek to accomplish.' . . . 'the State may not impose a blanket provision . . . requiring the consent of a parent or person *in loco parentis* as a condition for abortion of an unmarried minor.' . . . it is clear that Akron may not make a blanket determination that *all* minors under the age of 15 are too immature to make this decision or that an abortion never may be in the minor's best interests without parental approval . . . We do not think that the Akron ordinance, as applied in Ohio juvenile proceedings, is reasonably susceptible of being construed to create an 'opportunity for case-by-case evaluations of the maturity of pregnant minors.' . . . We therefore affirm the Court of Appeals' judgment that [the ordinance] is unconstitutional . . . In *Danforth, supra*, we upheld a Missouri law requiring a pregnant woman to 'certif[y] in writing her consent to the abortion and that her consent is informed and freely given and is not the result of coercion.' . . . The validity of an informed consent requirement thus rests on the State's interest in protecting the health of, the pregnant woman . . . This does not mean, however, that a State has unreviewable authority to decide what information a woman must be given before she chooses to have an abortion. It remains primarily the responsibility of the physician to ensure that appropriate information is conveyed to his patient, depending on her particular circumstances. *Danforth's* recognition of the State's interest in ensuring that this information be given will not justify abortion regulations designed to influence the woman's informed choice between abortion or childbirth. . . . We are not convinced, however, that there is a vital state need for insisting that the physician performing the abortion, or for that matter any physician, personally counsel the patient in the absence of a request. The State's interest is in ensuring that the woman's consent is informed and unpressured; the critical factor is whether she obtains the necessary information and counseling from a qualified person, not the identity of the person from whom she obtains it . . . In so holding, we do not suggest that the State is powerless to vindicate its interest in making certain that 'important' and 'stressful' decision to abort, 'is made with full knowledge of its nature and consequences.' . . . A State may define the physician's responsibility to include verification that adequate counseling has been provided and that the woman's consent is informed. In addition, the State may establish reasonable minimum qualifications for those people who perform the primary counseling function. . . . The Akron ordinance prohibit a physician from performing an abortion until 24 hours after the pregnant woman signs a consent form . . . We find that Akron has failed to demonstrate that any legitimate state interest is furthered by an arbitrary and inflexible waiting period. There is no evidence suggesting that the abortion procedure will be performed more safely . . . if a woman, after appropriate counseling, is prepared to give her written informed consent and proceed with the abortion, a State may not demand that she delay the effectuation of that decision."

Notes

Notes